MANDALA
AND THE
BUTTERFLY
SECRETS

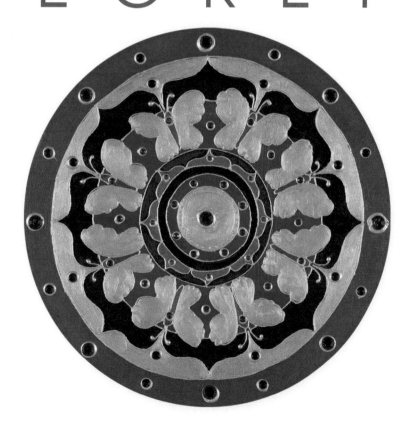

GINNYMARIE M. LEINES & RUTH M. GODFREY

Mandala and The Butterfly
SECRETS

iUniverse books may be ordered through booksellers or by contacting:

iUniverse
1663 Liberty Drive
Bloomington, IN 47403
www.iuniverse.com
844-349-9409

ISBN: 978-1-6632-1923-7 (sc)
ISBN: 978-1-6632-1922-0 (e)

Library of Congress Control Number: 2021904141

Print information available on the last page.

iUniverse rev. date: 08/03/2021

MANDALA
AND THE
BUTTERFLY
SECRETS

Artist & Illustrator Ginnymarie M. Leines

You Came to Me

You came to me.
Tiptoeing through my thoughts, my heart, my soul.
Secretly, you tightly held my gifts of hope and possibility.

I didn't realize the sacredness of what you had.
You were holding what matters.

I rejected you.
I said, "I'm not ready."

You ignored my pleas.
You choose
to walk alongside me,
pleading with me to listen.

One day you stopped walking.
You sat down.
You waited for my soul to catch up with me.
I missed you.
It was in this silence I heard your voice.

I began to understand
my dreams are who I am.
My dreams are the life in me.

—Ruth M. Godfrey

CONTENTS

FOREWORD

This is a book about the power of the human spirit and how we can handle any fallout when we focus on affecting our fate. As president of Learning Journeys, the International Center of Coaching, a designated ICF master certified coach and facilitator for coach training, I experience this phenomenon repeatedly with my clients and students. For over twenty years, I've had the opportunity to assist people in imagining and manifesting a life beyond their current situation. I'm still in awe every time I get to witness someone who musters up the strength to punch his or her circumstances in the face instead of surrendering to them. This is unbelievably hard work, and none of us are immune to the internal battles we experience while determining how to respond to our present status. In fact, there are many days when I and or my students fail to source our skills as we face our personal dilemmas. It is on these days that I pull out a piece I wrote awhile back. I read it out loud to my class to remind them, and myself, that if we remain fixed on the promise of a better future, we can endure the challenges of today.

The following is what I read:

A story is told of a caterpillar named Yellow who is trying to find out what she should be doing with her life. In her wanderings, she discovers another caterpillar seemingly caught in some gauzy, hairy filament. Concerned, she asks if she can help. He explains that this is all part of the process of becoming a butterfly. When she hears the word butterfly, her whole insides leap. "But, what is a butterfly?" The cocooned caterpillar explains, "It's what you are meant to become." Yellow is intrigued but a bit defiant. "How can I believe there's a butterfly inside you or me when all I see is a fuzzy worm?" On further reflection, she pensively asks, "How does one become a butterfly?" And the answer? "You must want to fly so much that you are willing to give up being a caterpillar."[1]

---

[1] Trina Paulus, *Hope for the Flowers* (New York: Paulist Press, 1972).

Every now and again, we find ourselves on a journey of transformation. When we are called to our adventure, we often resist at first. We do not have a clear idea of where we are headed and if our *there* will truly be better than our *here*. If we do not answer our call, we naturally focus on and fear what will end instead of shifting our perspectives to what will never get to begin.

The book *Hope for the Flowers* isn't just a bedtime story. Nature mimics real life. For a caterpillar to change into a butterfly, the shift is challenging and doesn't take form right away. The caterpillar's transformation begins with the appearance of scientists have termed *imaginal* cells.

At first, the imaginals are destroyed by the intelligence of the caterpillar organism. The imaginals keep coming back and eventually form clusters of cells to strengthen their domain. Soon the clusters form bonds where they pass genetic type information to one another. The clusters resonate at a higher frequency, beginning to change the physical makeup of the caterpillar. Eventually, the long string of clumping and clustering imaginal cells switches gears from being a group of likeminded cells into the programming cells of the butterfly. They literally reach a critical mass of influence where the caterpillar's destiny is altered to become a butterfly.

Researchers have no idea where these cells come from or why they appear. They are called imaginals because scientists hypothesize their purpose is to imagine something incredible is about to happen. We need to recognize when our inner resistance is trying to push away our dreams of an incredible future. Then we need to find ways to protect this image as we collect proof that our efforts are worthwhile. This will allow us to achieve our own critical mass and ultimately experience our awaited transformation.

We are the only species in the world with the gift of imagination. It allows us to ponder, predict, and even postpone our destinies. This book, through the sharing of stories, demonstrates the unstoppable strength we all possess when we utilize our imagination to envision and take action in the world we desire but doesn't quite yet exist.

—Jennie M. Antolak

INTRODUCTION

All people have dreams waiting to be nurtured. Sometimes, they fear acknowledging them.

To find happiness in life, you must leave your comfort zone to seek the unknowns of your future. The key to taking the risks to realize your dreams is to summon hope for a better future.

Hopes implies possibility. When we have hope, we open up, understanding what we desire is possible while not discounting the challenges we may face. When we have hope, it increases our chances of stepping into our dreams. It provides encouragement as we reach for our dreams. Hope requires us to believe in and trust in something we cannot see.

Dreams give our lives meaning. They heighten our ambitions, strengthen our identities, connect us to our values, and give us a sense of purpose and wonder. Having dreams inspires and fuels our passions.

In many ways, our lives are circular. In a spiritual sense, they are everlasting. Our physical bodies die. Our soulfulness lives on in the universe. In Sanskrit, the word *mandala* means circle. The geometric symbol is embraced in both the Hindu and Buddhist religion. It represents the spiritual journey of the soul that every self-actualized individual undertakes to reach his or her full potential. We are connected with everything in the universe, and if we understand and accept that, we can better understand how we fit into eternal existence. The mandala underlies the central premise of this book insofar as it serves as a focus for meditation, prayer, and inspiration. The butterfly in the title represents the power of mindfulness, transformation, and the endless possibilities that lie just over the horizon in all our lives.

Together, the mandala and the butterfly symbolize the power of our dreams. This is what the book is all about, helping you step into your dreams, creating a purposeful, hopeful, and rewarding life for you and the people you love.

This book is for you if you are

- searching for your dreams
- willing to take risks
- experiencing challenges
- wanting hope
- desiring a meaningful life
- fearful
- feeling lost
- dealing with the unexpected
- healing from within
- conflicted with inner and outer beauty
- meeting bullies head-on

As you explore the insights we present in the following pages, keep an open mind. Consider the stories from contributors illustrating core concepts creating understanding moving you to experience what we call the *Dream Flight*.

In addition to the stories, you'll find questions to ask yourself as you peel away the layers of resistance keeping you in a place you wish to leave. You'll find sections at the end of each chapter that summarize the lessons learned. In short, you have a handbook that will help you make the personal discoveries to give you the life you dream of.

You have the power to allow your dreams to come true. All you have to do now is take the first step on your *Dream Flight*.

CHAPTER 1

When Is the Right Time to Take Flight?

You came so that you could learn about your dreams, said the old woman. And dreams are the language of God. When He speaks in our language, I can interpret what He has said. But if He speaks in the language of the soul, it is only you who can understand.

—*The Alchemist*, Paulo Coelho

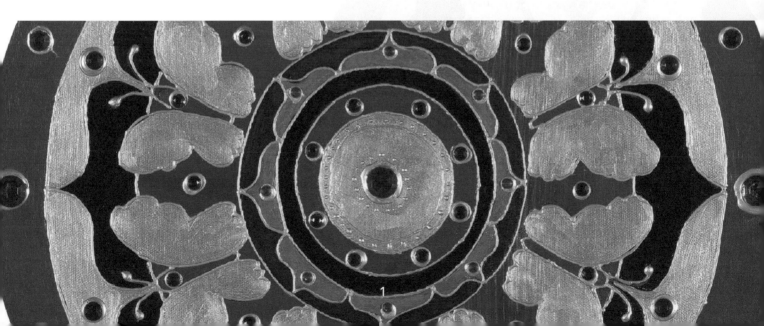

Mandala and The Butterfly

When we act on our dreams, we experience a sense of completeness in our lives.

Taking flight with our dreams grounds us in our passion and purpose. The mandala's circular design reflects this search for completeness. It represents the connection of our bodies, minds, and souls. Since the beginning of recorded history, mandalas have been discovered in ancient ruins. The mandala draws attention and purpose in every culture. Much like meditation, it gives us a sense of belonging as we allow ourselves to be in the moment, drawing on the thoughts and feelings that come. The mandala awakens our dreams and realizes possibility.

The Monarch butterfly travels four thousand miles to move to its warm winter home. The butterfly trusts its journey. It encourages and moves us with its resurrection as a caterpillar to the chrysalis to the majesty of a butterfly. This miraculous transformation creates hope for taking flight with our dreams.

As with everything else in the universe, a process unfolds as we make a conscious decision to pursue our dreams instead of ignoring them. This puts you intimately in touch with your thoughts, hopes, dreams, and desires. As noted in the introduction, this is the *Dream Flight*.

The Dream Flight

Be still.
Quiet your mind.
Be discerning.
Choose what is right for you.
Be trusting.
Tap into your inner wisdom.
Become your dreams.
Take action.

The following process works when you are searching for ways to manifest your dreams. Each action highlights strategies and behaviors designed to facilitate movement toward your dreams. We invite you to read each action and answer the reflective questions.

Action 1: Be Still

The goal of *be still* is to quiet your mind. It means to turn off the thoughts in your head in your head and be still. This will allow you to gain perspective and will lead you to your higher self while giving you room to notice what really matters in your life.

Reflective questions after you are still:

- What are you listening for?
- What are you hearing?
- Where are you being pulled?

Action 2: Be Discerning

The goal of *be discerning* is to arrive at the best decision when moving forward toward your dream. Discernment allows you to determine what is right for you. It is a way of making careful distinctions about the way you think about and interpret the world around you. It serves as a guide to seek the internal and external signs that point you toward your next step.

Reflective questions are useful when practicing discernment.

- What messages excite you?
- What are you making them mean?
- How do you want to respond?

Action 3: Be Trusting

The goal of *be trusting* is to be in tune with yourself. Listen to your inner wisdom. You have a sense of what is true and right for you. Trust it. When you trust yourself, you will have higher confidence in the core of who you are and who you are called to be.

Reflective questions are designed to reconfirm your inner wisdom.

- How can you trust your dreams are the reason you came to earth?
- What if you trust the time is now?
- How will you embrace your dreams when obstacles get in the way?

Action 4: Become Your Dreams

The goal of *become your dreams* is to stop waiting. Launch your dreams. Your dreams give meaning to your life. When you don't become your dreams, the whole world misses out. Imagine—when you become your dreams, you awaken others to their dreams. You will fulfill the reason you were sent to earth at this time. You leave a legacy for humanity.

Reflective questions designed to breathe life into your dreams:

- Who do you have to be to become your dreams?
- What bigger story for the world will they bring?
- How will your actions inspire others to live their dreams?

We know it is the right time to take flight when persistent nudges make us feel unsettled, ambivalent, and anxious. These signs call us to step over the threshold into our dreams. Mindset and perspective greatly influence the timeliness of taking flight with our dreams. They can dismantle creativity, eroding the possibility of our dreams. What if now is the right time to take flight with your dreams? Only you can know for sure; if you're reading this book, we think it's safe to say you're ready to soar.

Let's take a look at some stories that will help you as you create the courage it takes to actually act as opposed to sitting around thinking about doing something. The first story is from Ginnymarie.

Shoulda … Woulda … Coulda …

All I remember is running. I was running from one venue to the next in Tucson, Arizona. I was at the February Gem and Jewelry Show, on my first buying trip for my new business, Canyon Designs Jewelry & Objets d'Art. I had seen every possible precious gemstone imaginable, seen every genre of jewelry created throughout the world, and met worldwide artists. I was not ready to leave for my flight back to Salt Lake City.

I asked the cab driver if we could make one more stop. There was an old Howard Johnson's motel off the freeway exit. I wanted to check it out. I felt as if I was missing something. We rolled into the parking lot. I walked into the main atrium, where it was obvious the show was over. There weren't booths with vendors displaying. I could see two people and a table that looked empty at the other end of the atrium. I walked down and met George and JoAnn, from China. They were busy packing up their last box. It was rather big for jewelry. I asked if I could see what was in the boxes.

And that was it!

George pulled out a beautiful stone globe. It greeted me with strong energy. I asked to purchase the globe. Time was going way too fast. I had five more minutes before I would probably miss my flight. George would not sell me the globe. He had priced it at $1,000. He said he could create a globe for me.

He requested $1,000 up front. I pulled out a check, giving him the money on a handshake. He promised to contact me in the next two weeks.

Back in Salt Lake City, at my shop at Snowbird Ski and Summer Resort, I waited, and waited, and waited. From February until May, I waited. This was not the day of quick emails and international phone calls for pennies on the dollar. This was the day of fax machines, snail mail, and high-cost international calling. May came, and so did the fax. The globe was being shipped, and George and JoAnn were on their way to the States for another jewelry and gem show.

Would I like to meet them in California? I invited them to meet in Salt Lake City to discuss starting a manufacturing company. It was June. By September, I was importing containers of globes and shipping across North America. A container holds a thousand globes and takes thirty days to cross the ocean before it is in port.

It was the roaring '90s. The customers at the resort and retail outlets were enamored with the indigenous stones found in each country, carrying mysterious historical and cultural meaning. A shipping center was needed in Salt Lake City aside from our retail store to meet demand.

Business was growing exponentially, and delivery deadlines were tight. In late August, I flew to Hong Kong, focusing my time in the jewelry district in Kowloon. I wanted to experience the artistry and review manufacturing systems. I rode the bus inland to our manufacturing and artisan center. Long blonde hair to my waist, simple flowing clothes to soothe the effects of high humidity, rain, and one hundred-degree temperatures attracted attention in this country of small, strong, narrow builds and black hair. People on the bus were wanting to touch my hair. They pointed at me and said, "Movie star."

During our two-hundred-mile trip, our bus pulled over three times by Chinese police. The bus stopped, everyone filed out, I was escorted to a small building, my computer was turned on, and I was asked, "What is on your computer?" Each time, I showed the computer was my travel companion to communicate with people in the States.

Arriving at the center was an experience unlike anything in my life. Night had come, I was informed *absolutely not* to leave the hotel alone. George and his assistant came to meet me. They drove an old New Yorker with the back window curtained. They were so proud of their American car. We drove through crowded streets with barred garage doors open. Many housed ping-pong tables with old black-and-white TVs playing American sitcoms from the '80s. This was the Chinese perspective on how Americans live; old sitcoms, short miniskirts, high boots. We arrived at the gates. A guard waved us through. At that moment, a horrific explosion occurred. It was not an explosion. It was four stories of fireworks lit in my honor as a gesture of prosperity and unity.

The next day, we ventured back to the center, where George gave me a tour. There were one hundred and fifty people working with one couple as the designated cooks. No children. They were separated from their parents and left with relatives in the country. The artisans worked three months and then went back to their families and children for six weeks. This was their work cycle.

George had a big old-world city-newspaper-style office from the 1950s. His interior office windows were draped with dirty, faded curtains. He watched his secretaries spying on them like a hawk. He wore a white shirt, proper pants, and polished shoes. These clothes were purchased to impress me. They cost more than one month's wages. He had his secretaries dress like "Americans." They were dressed in straight short miniskirts with stiletto-heeled thigh high boots and red lipstick.

We proceeded to lunch, made using an electric wok and a fifty-five-gallon drum of water for washing vegetables, hands, and utensils. I smiled, taking a deep breath. I was hesitant to eat soup with floating fish eyes, dumplings, and something disguised as vegetables. They were proud of their food. They hugged me.

After finishing our meal, we walked out to eight-foot-high piles of raw lapis rocks the size of small turtles, dumped haphazardly in the center of the courtyard. Upstairs, in the finishing room, worked a man in his twenties. His biceps and triceps bulged unnaturally. They looked like registered weapons. He shaped the final globe using a handheld grinder. He worked seven days a week, ten to twelve hours a day, for three months, without a break. A bathroom break consisted of going to a drafty, dirty room with a hole in the floor, no toilet paper, and a fifty-five-gallon barrel of water. This water was used for washing vegetables as well as kitchen utensils. One hundred and fifty people shared the barrel. Water was in short supply. The water was replaced once a week.

My stay was filled with gratitude for the hard work and kindness of my artisans. It was an immense effort to begin and complete one globe. Women in their eighties and nineties worked the same hours as young people.

My globe idea for the Denver Bronco World Champion Dinner Team Celebration was awarded. I secured rights to manufacture the Denver Broncos horse head with a diamond for each eye, diamonds placed in each country the team played in, and a poured globe stand with "Denver Broncos, World Champions," printed on it. I had a twelve-week deadline to deliver more than one hundred and fifty globes. I created a five-foot-diameter surprise globe, to be delivered at the event for John Elway. The pressure was on. Years later, I watched a John Elway special interview at his home. There, before me, on the big screen, was the very large globe, a prized Elway possession. I felt excited, ambivalent, and disappointment.

Looking back, it is easy to find answers to the shoulda … woulda … coulda … for success. Great momentum, early success, and good organizational and marketing skills did not prepare me for a sudden shift in pricing, availability, manufacturing terms, and dishonesty from my business partners.

The dream chased and found me giving many great moments of travel to China. For a long time, I lacked trust and faith in pursuing partnerships and collaboration. I learned the importance of taking care of legal accountability upfront. I learned how handshakes are only as good as the integrity of the individual. I learned words are empty without commitment. It taught me: be still, be discerning, be trusting in new ways, and know that becoming my dreams is a undulating path.

—Ginnymarie

How I Became a Mother in Thirty Seconds

Seventeen years ago, David and Carol purchased a home in dire need of renovation and repairs. Carol saw the house as a creative project drawing on her resources and imagination. Today, their home is fully restored. It can be found on the St. Louis, Missouri, Historical Registry. Carol is drawing on her motherhood business experiences, participating in environmental restoration projects within her city. Now a grandmother, Carol has seen her own children grow up to enjoy families of their own. Carol lives in St. Louis, Missouri, with her husband, David. Here's her story about finding the grit and courage it takes to actively pursue a dream. In her case, her dream involved giving up a prosperous business out of a moral sense of goodness toward children in need. In short, she sacrificed for others, and in the end, she came out on top.

When is the right time to take flight? Carol said it was when her gut whispered, "Yes," and her head screamed, "No!"

Carol heard a knock on her front door. Opening the door, she found a frightened six-year-old boy looking up at her. Carol looked around for his mother. She was gone. The boy was Carol's stepson Doug, looking bewildered and afraid. She wrapped her arms him and brought him into the house. She felt like crying for him. A week later, the same thing happened again. Her two-year-old stepdaughter, Kim, was dropped off at her front door. Unexpectedly, Carol became the fulltime mother for her two stepchildren. She was willing to fail to succeed at motherhood.

She believed God placed her stepchildren into her hands because they needed her. She felt becoming the children's mother was her ultimate responsibility.

Carol dreamed about having children someday with her husband, David. Her dream came true.

Carol and David wrestled with readjusting their lives becoming a family of four. They decided taking care of them needed one parent's full attention. She found her business was diverting her attention from the children. She sold her company and embraced a new business, motherhood.

Her head told her, "No!"

Carol's gut told her, "This will be your journey!"

She discovered her kids had traumatic emotional issues. She found family counseling resources and friends who helped her and her family during their darkest hour. Carol relied on her entrepreneurial skills to find answers and understand the children's well-being.

Carol became immersed in her new business of motherhood. God's gift taught her how to live in the moment focusing right where she was.

"Why have children if you don't answer the knock on your door?"

Carol knows there will be a new knock on her door someday. She is ready to greet whoever is on the other side. The lesson is that we don't know what is coming tomorrow. However, we can decide how we want to be ready.

We give flight to our dreams by holding steadfast to our willingness to fail.
—Carol Ann Docken Fisher

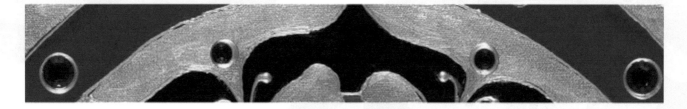

My Near-Death Experience

Torsten Jon Leines is a business owner, entrepreneur, professional golfer, and former member of the US Snowboarding Team. Torsten holds a Bachelor of Science degree in Economics from the University of Utah, Salt Lake City. He cherishes time spent on the lake with family and friends, having a BBQ and sharing funny jokes. Torsten treasures family above all else and asks himself, *How will this decision affect my family and our future?* He is a practitioner of power yoga. Here is his story.

When is the right time to take flight with one's most cherished dreams? Torsten said, "It was right after my crash landing. Flying through the air after impact felt like time had stopped. It was like watching a movie, except I was the main character."

Torsten was on his way to class at the University of Utah. The short walk brought him to a crosswalk. He looked left up the street. No cars were coming. He looked right, down the street. It was a steep hill. He walked across to the middle, looking right again to check for cars coming up the hill.

Bang!

Jerked up into the air, he had gone through the windshield of a car. He heard glass break, and he was in the air. His cowboy boots, neatly tucked under his jeans and over long underwear, were ripped off. They were left standing upright as though someone had carefully placed them on the street. His eyes caught horrified expressions of people seeing him fly past them as they looked out the window of their morning bus ride to work.

Torsten flew 85 feet through the air. He bounced over and over again on the pavement until his body came to rest. The arriving officer at the scene asked for witnesses, observing Torsten was unconscious. The response surprised him when Torsten, covered in blood, called out, "I am your witness." He did not lose consciousness. This miraculous gift was a result of his athletic training for his snowboarding competitions. His brain suffered a serious concussion.

Numerous surgeries later, he was released from the hospital in a wheelchair. In one millisecond, Torsten went from being a college student and nationally ranked athlete to facing the physical, mental, and emotional challenges of being struck on a crosswalk by a speeding car, driven by a distracted driver. Torsten learned to walk, recovering from a serious concussion, and regaining his former USSA snowboarding athletic self.

Post-traumatic stress disorder would haunt him. He would be sitting on the couch when a playback of flying through the air and feeling like a ragdoll would overcome him. The facial expressions of horrified passengers on the bus appeared out of nowhere.

Torsten started working with Rich, a personal trainer, twice a week to maximize his physical therapy and dig into coping with PTSD. Their goal was to develop self-discipline and focus for

Torsten's future. Rich became Torsten's confidante and dear friend. Rich introduced Torsten to the book *The Way of the Peaceful Warrior*. Torsten believes Rich was a true peaceful warrior. Together, they drew on the book's peaceful-warrior paradigm of being time-tested and pain sharpened. Their focus was recognizing that heaven is within and living well with honor, courage, and compassion for all people. During his mentorship, Rich was diagnosed with a rare form of terminal cancer that would take his life six months later. Rich was in his thirties. Torsten was alone. It would be up to him to carry out the quest of his peaceful warrior.

"Now" is his motto. Excuses are not accepted. It is his motto for moving into action with a clear vision for realizing a dream. Day after day, Torsten worked at building up muscle strength, flexibility, and the steps to walking again. He was sitting in his wheelchair one day when his friend showed up with a golf green. He rolled it out in the great room.

Within two years, Torsten became a two scratch golfer. His body did not allow him to snowboard with one leg shorter than the other and residual injury limitations. He put his sights on playing on the PGA Tour. He missed the sectional US Open qualifying by 2 strokes twice.

Love, his future family, and business took precedence over a golf career. He had a dream from childhood to work with his father in the energy business. Today, Torsten draws on the knowledge and experiences he had growing up and working with his father. He maps out his plan on his office white board. He is a man of action with research, vision, and possibility as his closest allies. His work ethic, focused training, and belief draw on his competitive history at the Intermountain Snowboard venues, Nationals, and US Open to fulfill his dreams. Getting hit by a car on a crosswalk and losing his dear friend and recovery mentor further opened his eyes to the importance of reaching for his dreams every day. He draws on his peaceful-warrior practices, remembering that "now" is the time to act and heaven is within him.

When I stare down the fairway, I visualize the intended line of flight of the golf ball. My preparation of execution is defined. The probability of the outcome becomes closer to my world vision.
—Torsten Jon Leines

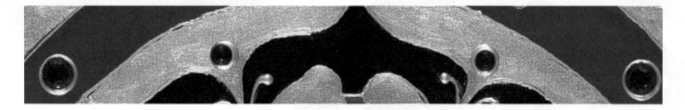

My Daughter's Rare Genetic Condition

Deb Dubois is a master certified coach and narrative coach practitioner. She is an innovative marketer with twenty-five years experience in the industry. She partners with clients to build brands and resolve business challenges, creating new business growth. She lives in the heart of downtown Minneapolis, Minnesota. Her friends nicknamed her "Downtown Deb." Deb continues to serve as an advocate for people with disabilities.

Recently, both Deb and her daughter, Mary, participated in the National Policies and Partnership training to influence and inform the legislature and senate on laws that are harmful to the disabled population while also directing them to what does work.

When Deb gave birth to Mary, the doctors said Mary would never live past the age of four. How wrong they were. That was thirty years ago. Today, Mary is an advocate for herself and others who have a disability.

When Deb sees an injustice, regardless if it affects herself or others, she is not intimated by people who have the power to make decisions related to disability laws. Instead, she becomes informed. She becomes a loud voice, attempting to inform others about the adverse impact of their decisions.

Mary is missing chromosome 8p. Every human cell typically has twenty-three pairs of chromosomes. The exact cause for a missing chromosome was unknown. Even today science doesn't know what causes the deficiency; nor do they have the means to treat it, which makes the genetic condition rare. In fact, worldwide only 350 people share this condition.

There are all kinds of health ramifications for patients missing the 8p chromosome. In Mary's case, it caused delayed developmental issues. From the moment Mary was born, her quality of life was compromised. For example, she didn't have the strength in her mouth to chew food, she could not focus her eyes, and her hearing was impaired. She would hear something different from what was being presented to her. Sitting and walking were developmentally delayed. As a family, they had no idea what was next for Mary. At the same time, they feared asking for advanced medical care. They were worried the insurance company would drop their insurance coverage.

Deb has learned to navigate complex medical systems, attempting to find answers for Mary as various health issues continue to confront her. Deb told us the big question she faces as the mother of an adult child is, "How do I provide guidance and care when your adult child deserves and demands her own voice, her own independence?" Mary is a brave, outspoken woman who has learned to be an advocate for herself. She continues to persevere without wondering or caring what others think. Today, Mary is in her midthirties. Her complex chromosomal differences affect her well-being every day—difficulty digesting foods, abdominal pain, difficulty walking, and impaired vision. Recognizing a strong desire in Mary to be independent, Deb steps back even when Mary is battling a difficult issue. Deb trusts and allows her daughter to be a voice for herself. As a mother, Deb realizes that Mary's demands are no different from those of other young adults. Deb is challenged by wanting to respect her daughter's desire for independence. Deb believes it is the utmost importance that she oversee her care as a vulnerable adult.

Deb shared, "Sometimes I feel overwhelmed with the medical concerns, staff, and apartment challenges, as well as activities of Mary's daily living needs." She went onto say that glimmers of hope are present everywhere. Mary's desire for independence is a force onto itself.

When Mary's doctors felt she needed to go to a nursing home, they believed Mary's health was more than what she could manage on her own. Mary's solution was to have a personal-care attendant. However, there is a shortage of personal-care attendants in Minnesota who are available to make home visits. If she were to be placed in a nursing home, her doctors believed she would receive the medical care she needed. Mary resisted the idea. She cherishes her independence. Plus, she would no longer be with people her own age. She informed them, "No, I am not going to a nursing home." Mary stood her ground by appealing to Minneapolis Hennepin County Social Services. Mary used her appeal rights. Recently, the appeals division of the Minnesota Department of Human Services ruled in Mary's favor. Mary did this without her mother's knowledge.

The lesson we can learn is never underestimate a person with a disability. When Mary wants something and thinks she has the tools and voice to be heard, she uses them. She is reminding us not to give up on what we want and to keep moving forward.

Deb's experience with her daughter has inspired her to become an advocate for people with disabilities. Her mission in life is to be a guiding influence in shaping laws that affect people with disabilities. These laws offer the best possible life experiences. Deb sees a need for a shared understanding of the complexities unique to this special population.

Mary continues to motivate Deb to live her life from a place of trust and determination.

Deb expressed gratitude for the gift Mary has been in her life. She said, "She brings out the best in our friends as well as other parents, family, medical specialists, teachers, social-services professionals, and volunteers who nurture and love her. We don't know what's next. We will hear Mary's voice and will honor her decisions. It's her life and her story. I am Mary's mother, and that is my story."

Life is a complicated journey filled with ups and downs. I have learned that when I am down, it is not necessarily about me.
—Deb DuBois

Great Questions to Ask

- What tells you it is the right time to take flight with your dreams?
- Where will you go?
- Who will be your travel companions?

_____

_____

_____

_____

_____

_____

_____

_____

_____

_____

_____

_____

_____

_____

_____

_____

Themes, Core Concepts, and Lessons Learned

- There are signs all around alerting us to take flight.
- Mindset and perspective greatly influence us.
- We must be mindful of our thoughts.
- Although it may be scary, finding the courage to take action is a vital first step toward taking flight.

Chapter Notes and Resources

In Wilson's book, he stated,

> Research reveals three key ingredients that make us happy. They are meaning, hope and purpose. He goes onto say we will always experience spills, tumbles, hassles, and setbacks in life. When we are in a state of uncertainty and are facing the unexpected it is important to understand what has occurred.

Wilson highlights the importance of making sense of situations, giving them meaning and purpose. He reminds the reader we have the capability to step back and observe our experiences. When we do, we are more able to have a healthy response.

We concluded from the key messages in Wilson's book that when unexpected situations occur, we have the power to bear witness to self, others, and the world around us. This requires a willingness to *be still* and *be discerning*. Be still and be discerning became part of our learning model: the D*ream Flight*.

Wilson, Timothy D. *Redirect: Changing the Stories We Live By*. New York: Back Bay Books, 201be.

CHAPTER 2

What Happens When a Dream Catches You?

Your dream will find you. It is what it is. You can hide from it. You can hold hands with it. You can cover it up with a blanket. It will still find you.
—Heidi Tuneberg

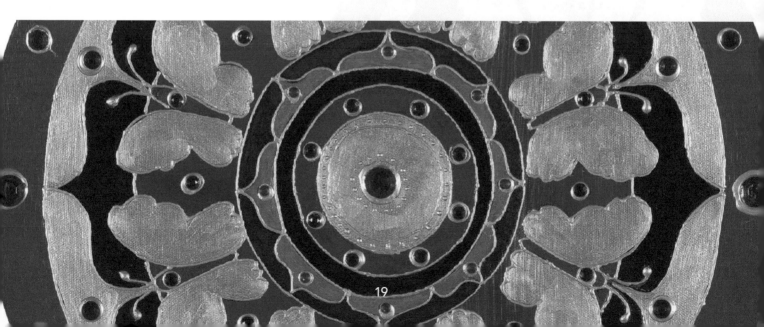

19

Mandala and The Butterfly

A dream catches a butterfly before it has an idea what flying is or what navigational challenges the winter season will demand. During the chrysalis stage of development, the butterfly moves toward its dream of becoming. It does this with abandonment and hope. Their dream is calling them to become a butterfly. You are called to trust and follow your dreams. This is how transformation takes place. The butterfly reminds you to keep your faith as you experience your transformation.

Imagine a mandala speaking to a butterfly. What if he asks, "How can you be brave when you have no idea what the outcome will be?"

Without hesitation, the Butterfly answers, "Oh, beautiful mandala, I don't have a choice. My dream has captured my soul."

This is your message from the mandala and butterfly. You can choose to embrace hope and draw on the mandala to imagine and visualize the great wonder of your dreams. Your dreams live within you, asking to be embraced.

Trust your inner knowing when a dream catches you. It is there for a reason. You can take a second look. You can step out of your chrysalis, thank the threshold behind you, and take flight. When you have retreated into your personal chrysalis, it is your imaginary protection and safeguard, closing off your dreams. How can you step out of your chrysalis and trust your dreams are calling you? Here's what happened to Ruthie.

A Dream Caught Me

"Ruthie, catch!"

I turned toward the person calling my name, reached up, and caught a magazine in midair. This is how a dream came to me. I was working at the Metropolitan Waste Control, which is now the Metropolitan Council. We employed about 1,500 people. The legislature had changed the organization, merging us with several service agencies.

This created employment for four thousand people. We found ourselves with three separate human resource departments. It was determined this would not work. Each employee was asked to reapply for their job. I was one of them. I experienced anger, hurt, anxiety, nausea, and fear.

Out of nowhere, a magazine appeared, and my life was changed forever. When I arrived at work and hung up my coat, I put my laptop on my desk. I walked to the Public Relations department to grab a cup of coffee. I talked with the PR team before I went back to my office.

Our company was being dismantled. Many of my colleagues received pink slips. They arrived at work to find a pink slip sitting on their chair. The pink slip became the new employee. They had been replaced.

A temp agency provided the company with an administrative assistant. She was the one who threw me the magazine. When she told me to catch it, she said, "Look at the cover. I think that could be you."

How did she know? It will always remain a puzzle to me. I never saw her again after that day. The magazine was the latest publication of *Minnesota Monthly*. On the cover was a picture of a woman named Valerie Olson. The caption read, "Life Coach, an Up and Coming Career."

I took the magazine, grabbed my coffee, and walked back to my office, intrigued by the caption. I can remember the feeling of excitement running through my body as I read Valerie's story. When I finished the article, I had to know more. I looked up Valerie's phone number. I invited her to meet with me for lunch.

When we met, I had a million questions about how she got started, what she loved about it, how she saw coaching as a viable business, and so on. The more we talked, the more I knew this was exactly what I was being called to do. I discovered a life coach is a professional who partners with others to achieve their dreams.

I hired Valerie that evening. I enrolled in the coaching certification program she recommended. The rest is history. I completed the certification. I enrolled in a different coaching certification headed by Peter Redding at Coach for Life. This was for my master certification. The last piece for certification was the oral exam.

I was feeling anxious. I was in San Diego. Peter invited me for dinner to take my oral exam. I couldn't enjoy dinner with the exam looming over me. I summoned the courage to ask Peter if I could complete the exam before dinner. Peter reached across the table and handed me the test questions.

When I got to the third question, Peter did something that startled me. He reached for my test and tore it up. I was mortified, believing I had failed miserably. Peter said, "Ruthie, go back to Minnesota and start your own school. You know coaching inside and out." Release permeated my body. I had passed.

I went back to Minnesota. My daughter, Jennie, picked me up at the airport. I shared with her what happened. She said, "Mom, I am all in."

Since 2000, we have owned and operated the International Center of Coaching, Learning Journeys. Today, we are a licensed post-secondary school. Our Level One program is accredited by the International Coach Federation. In addition, we are an approved Veterans Administration coaching-certification provider for those who have served our country.

We never know what may be waiting for us on the cover of a magazine.

—Ruthie

I Got Down on My Knees

Scott Kearns favorite moments are spent with fiancée, Monique Dionne. As a chef, he takes pride in creating a meaningful Sunday brunch. Personal development and public speaking are his trademarks, connecting at the heart level. He is a sought-after international motivational speaker. He holds a bachelor of science degree in pharmacology from the University of Western Ontario. Scott is the number-one direct sales leader and business developer in Canada for Isagenix. Scott was nominated for the Canadian 2018 Isagenix Man of the Year Award. He lives in Toronto, Canada. This is his story.

Scott says he allowed his inner dreams, the ones he ignored for years, to ignite his passion for change only after he pushed away his negative self-talk and got down on his knees. Scott's internal struggle was cloaked by trappings of his ego. How he felt inside was his nemesis. He felt handcuffed by anxiety. He felt trapped in a caged cell. He felt captive, like a prisoner to his past.

Scott experienced an epiphany when he flew to South Korea to build his business. He met a man who was a single parent of two young children. When the man met Scott, he said, "You are my answer to prayer." Scott invited him to join his business. Today, they work together in their international business.

Six months later, Scott was working with clients in California. His phone pinged. He had a text. It was a woman he met in South Korea who had a business in California. She asked if he would be able to connect with her. She was in San Diego. Scott was in San Francisco. He felt excited and nervous. In Korea, she was not interested in taking a deeper look at Scott's business. A short flight later, they sat down to discuss their overseas meeting. Today, they are in partnership, growing a new branch of business together.

Scott asked himself, *Why did I think I could go to South Korea and build my business?* He found his answer. It was God's plan not his. Anxiety and fear poked at him. He kept with his plan to go to South Korea.

Today, he has chosen to course-correct his business pursuits rather than compromise his inner knowing—God's plan. Scott can't see it. Belief is his choice.

Scott's foundation for life is a metaphor. It is symbolic of an immense boulder. Solid and heavy, it can only be moved by a miraculous force. *Force majeure*, an act of God.

Fear will not steer my ship any longer. God will.
—Scott Kearns

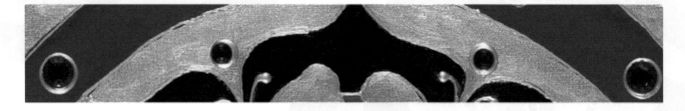

Their Pain Became My Pain

Judy Zimmer is the president and founder of Coachology, a coaching and speaking firm. Judy is known for her personal branding expertise and executive presence coach business. She is a watercolor exhibitor and commissioned artist. Judy lives in Minneapolis, Minnesota.

Judy realized her dreams when she opened her mind to an idea that touched her soul. You might say the dream came to find her. She wasn't actively searching for change in her life, but she was struggling with a big question as she worked on ways to feed the hungry.

How do you find a way to feed 1,800 kids? How do you find a way to feed 20,000 kids? Internally moved by the fact there are children in the United States who go to sleep hungry every night, Judy searched for a solution. She told herself, *many movements have started with one person.* She wondered, *Can I be the one?*

When she was mulling over the question, she held another dream in the forefront of her mind. It was a more personal dream. She imagined standing on stage speaking before an audience of 20,000 people or more. For years, she held onto that dream, and then, one day, she felt unsure if the dream held the same passion for her. She realized feeding children held a bigger place in her heart than professional speaking. She asked herself, *Does this dream still make sense? How will it serve others?* She soon became aware the dream was more complex than she had imagined. Her speaking engagements could offer the financial solution to what she now perceived her more urgent and bigger goal—to feed the children. The following year, she was able to donate to three charities that fed 1,800 children, all because of the monies she earned from her speaking engagements. Judy has designed a business model donating to a charity each time she has a new speaking contract.

Since she has stepped into what she believes is her bigger dream, Judy has discovered there are many, many more children who go hungry every day in the USA. She is on track to feed 20,000 children every year and is inspired to serve more in the years to come. Judy's quest is to be that one person who makes a difference in the world. Her favorite quote is

> Never forget that you are one of a kind. Never forget that if there wasn't any need for you in all your uniqueness to be on this earth, you wouldn't be here. And never forget, no matter how overwhelming life's challenges and problems seem to be, that one person can make a difference in the world. In fact, it is always because of one person that all the changes that matter in the world come about. So be that one person.
> —Buckminister Fuller, architect, engineer, inventor

I have a sense of belonging when I feel comfortable in my own skin. Then I serve people better. I find I ask bigger questions, learn more about them, and share my joy. It is at that moment I contribute to the world.
—Judy Zimmer

The Dark Side of My Teenage Feelings

Dr. Glenn Nemec is a thoughtful, gifted family physician who volunteers annually, bringing medical care to people lacking modern technologies and medical services in the Caribbean. He has practiced medicine in Monticello, Minnesota, for the past thirty years. He is the president of the Minnesota Academy of Family Practice. He is married to Caren. They have two adult children, Gregg and Jacqueline, and one adorable grandson, Liam. Dr. Nemec is active in Lions Club International, his home church congregation, and Medical Mission International, through Mission Jamaica. He loves outdoor sports, with scuba diving and skiing being his personal favorites. Dr. Nemec is an avid reader of science fiction. He lives in Big Lake, Minnesota.

Glenn's story illustrates how dreams can nudge you when you least expect it. They lurk in the background of your thoughts, and they poke and push gently, and sometimes not so gently, until you pay attention to them. When you do, you've got a choice to make. Do you act on your dreams, or do you shove them back into the closet and lock the door?

Glenn looks back on his life to trace the origins of the dreams that shaped him as an individual.

What is it about adolescence that paints a picture of angst, frustration, and awkwardness? Living through the teen years is rarely met with the desire for a chance to do it again. He said, as a teenager, his feelings ran deep. His responses to them were fast. He created one "bad" experience after another.

Enter the world of *Star Trek* and Mr. Spock. This was Dr. Nemec's favorite TV series. Mr. Spock had something Dr. Nemec wanted. Mr. Spock had full control and mastery of his emotions. Dr. Nemec modeled himself after Mr. Spock. He watched every *Star Trek* episode, over and over, to figure out how to be like Mr. Spock. After many failed attempts, Dr. Nemec began to realize how things could be different when he mastered his emotions. As he grew into an adult, he found his power and inner peace. He knew he could choose not to react but instead step back and process his feelings before responding. Dr. Nemec chose to push negativity away to create pause and positivity for finding a solution in the moment.

Unlike Mr. Spock, Dr. Nemec's bigger challenge is the human conundrum. Like Mr. Spock, he learned to separate himself from circumstances to scan his environment and determine what was occurring around him. This self-discipline has become the capstone for Dr. Nemecs' community and medical leadership.

Mr. Spock's father gave him sage advice upon beginning his adult journey. Dr. Nemec's father did the same for him. When he left for medical school, his father's advice, which continues to guide him today, was, as you learn about the science of the human body and how it works, take a step back and try to convince yourself that something this wonderful could really happen by accident. This became the foundation for Dr. Nemec's medical-school journey. His father's philosophy continues to reinforce his belief that there are things going on in this world that are not of this world.

Secrets in Life
FUN!!
Fun is way under-rated,
Live it.
SERVICE!!
Help someone else
It is the best remedy
for whatever is bothering you.
—Dr. Glenn Nemec

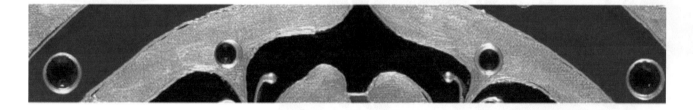

Alone in Open Waters

Kristen Bor is the founder of Bearfoot Theory Media Company. She is a freelance writer and photographer. Her contributions include the Pew Charitable Trusts, Senior Associate, Legislative Associate-Natural Resources, Project Management UCSB Economic Viability/Fishing Community, PADI Open Water Scuba Instructor, Thailand, University of Puget Sound, BS in Chemistry. UC Santa Barbara, master's degree, Environmental Science and Management. Kristen lives in Salt Lake City, Utah.

As you can see from Kristen's credentials, she's into the great outdoors, but she wasn't always. Here's the story of how her dreams evolve.

Imagine what it would be like to be an open-water master scuba-dive instructor on the coast of Thailand, a deckhand in Hawaii, a solo backpacker across Indonesia, and a lobby conservationist in Washington, D.C. Until Kristen went to Hawaii, her interest in spending time in nature wasn't part of her life.

Once she attained her dream job in Washington, she became disillusioned, restless, and unhappy. She knew this was not what her internal messenger was telling her. The job was affecting her sense of self. She felt as if she would never fulfill her dream to explore the world. She traveled for her job. Her time was spent in boardrooms without windows. She took flight after flight to great cities around the world. However, she went from the airport to meetings. Exploring her destination was not part of her job description.

It was the impetus to look at travel blogs and jobs that could engage her travel dream. She enrolled in a one-on-one mentorship program to further her search. The dream unfolded as Kristen created a clear vision of what she wanted to do. She developed her idea to become an outdoor-adventure role model for women. She quit her job and founded Bearfoot Theory. *Forbes*, *Outside*, and *Outdoor Adventure* magazines have featured stories about Kristen's blog creation, lifestyle, environmental contribution, and fiscal success. When the dream caught Kristen, she fully embraced accountable steps to frame her vision.

Bearfoot Theory became her blog name and her travel and business companion.

Within the span of five years, she created a full-time staff of contributors who partner with her to help more people get outside and get in touch with nature. The *Bearfoot Theory* website is designed for women to help them overcome fears and build confidence in their outdoor adventures. It assists them in putting together the best possible gear for every experience. Kristen's blog shares her favorite destinations, gear, and tips for living a more adventuresome life for everyday people who want to travel the globe.

It doesn't happen overnight. You must work like crazy. I'm living proof it's completely possible to build something from nothing.
—Kristen Bor

The X Games Called Me

Erik Jon Leines is an entrepreneur and professional athlete. He is a world renowned snowboarder, winning second place in the nation at the age of twelve. Erik was a US Snowboarding Team member, US Open Competitor, X Games Competitor, and under contract for over fifteen years with many industry companies, including Oakley, Ride, Vans, and Smith Goggles. Erik is cofounder of CELTEK, worldwide distributor and international manufacturer of soft goods for snowboarders and skiers. They developed supply chains and established a global sales infrastructure. As merchandise manager for Stance Socks, he helped the company achieve $100 million in revenue in 2018. He was the global senior merchandising manager for DC Shoe Company. Erik loves snowboarding and surfing. He is married to Ashley Stewart. Together they own their family business, Stewart Surfboards, founded by Bill and Chris Stewart forty years ago. Erik and Ashley have three daughters, Emianna, Vivia, and Ellery. They live in San Clemente, California.

Erik's story reveals how a sense of excitement and adventure can lead to dreaming big. Erik says, "Let the adventure begin." Let's start with his snowboarding.

Erik strapped into his snowboard, focused his mind and pushed off. He felt relief and excitement successfully completing his run on the uninviting surface manufactured for the event. Earlier in the morning, trucks filled with ice chips had parked along the ramp area. The projectile ice chips took the place of mountain snow on the Oceanside Mission Bay, a California X Games venue. Thousands of people milled around, with DJ music rocking out, vendors, photographers, and news people. They had no idea of the real danger nearby. Blasts of strong winds came up. The scaffold pitched forward, sinking a foot into the sandy beach. There was a sudden moment of silence. The ESPN X Games announcer called out for the fans' attention.

Erik's call to the X Games was interrupted. All snow events were cancelled. The crowd of X Games fans moved on down the beach. Erik took off his snowboard boots, slipped into Reef flip-flops, and walked back to the Oakley House around the corner. The celebration for the first-ever "Snow" Summer X Games was on at the Oakley House.

Competition for a place on the podium was over this time.

Erik's dream to become a professional snowboard competitor was realized at a young age. Focused and disciplined, Erik dedicated his teen years to training on the mountain, on dry land, and on mental acuity. After competing for a decade, he started looking at an exit strategy within the industry to continue his love of snowboarding.

Erik and his brother, Bjorn, launched their company, CELTEK, a journey into global business. It is a design, manufacturing, and distribution corporation. During the development phase of CELTEK,

Erik spent two years seeking investors to collaborate and grow the brand. Oftentimes, Erik was met with an attitude of prejudice as a professional athlete. During his late twenties and into his thirties, he separated himself from his athletic accomplishments, vying to overcome this prejudice. Erik shared that he did not want to be treated with disdain because he was a professional athlete. At the same time, he didn't want preferential treatment for his achievements. His new dream was to become recognized as an entrepreneur.

Erik came full circle. Today, he walks tall in his celebration and ownership of his professional snowboarding career, alongside his distinctive drive as an entrepreneurial businessman. He shared great respect for his sense of belonging, to the tribe, the extended family culture within the industry, and the different company's team riders, and he related how this has been an unexpected gift from his snowboarding career.

Living the Golden Rule creates a path of celebration for me.
—Erik Jon Leines

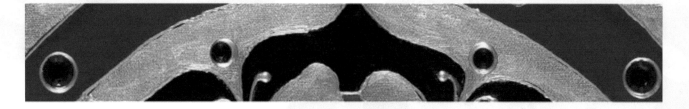

Great Questions to Ask

- When have dreams found you?
- What happened?
- What surprised you?

Themes, Core Concepts, and Lessons Learned

- A dream will always be waiting for you to take action.
- Trust your inner knowing when a dream catches you.
- Be open and ready to respond.

Chapter Notes and Resources

Our dreams are calling us to take a risk. New research on the genetic component relating to why certain people take risks has found that their genetic makeup is correlated to behaviors. It is the role of specific genes that regulate neurotransmitters, affecting chemical messengers that stimulate and calm the brain. The study discovered that an individual's environment combined with their genetic makeup affected their risk-taking choices.

Kurlsson Liner, Richard, Birool, Petro, and Beachemp, Jonathan P. "Genetic-wide association analysis of risk tolerance." *Nature Genetics Journal,* January 14, 2019.

CHAPTER 3

What Gets in the Way of Soaring High?

My fear gets in the way of soaring high.
—Denielle Jones

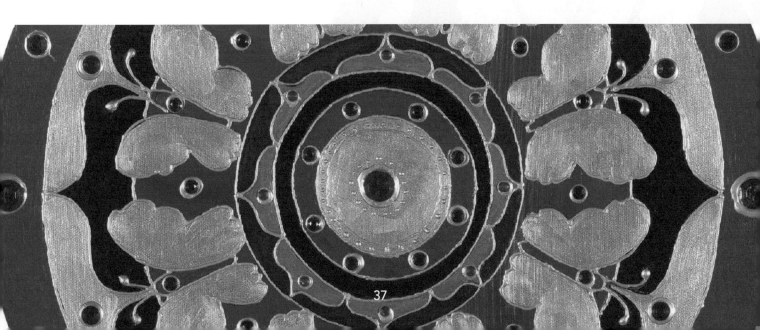

Mandala and The Butterfly

Thinking about a mandala and butterfly can help you understand what is getting in the way of soaring high with your dreams. The mandala creates a space to get out of your head and into your heart. This can be experienced through meditation or prayer, using the mandala as a visual influence. This practice gives you an opportunity to gracefully let go of the old to embrace the new. The mandala helps you act on what you know. The butterfly greets you as a caterpillar. It symbolizes hope. It is a necessary component to becoming a butterfly. The same is true when you allow circumstances to get in the way of soaring high. The chrysalis literally provides the butterfly with cellular matter, insuring its destiny to take flight. Without it, there cannot be a butterfly. You travel along the path of the caterpillar seeking the essence of the mandala as you camp in the space of indecision or are confronted by obstacles within your journey.

Fear is a powerful force. Fear, in every form, is the number-one reason given by our contributors why they get stalled out from fulfilling their dreams. Fear carries power unless it is confronted with confidence. It is a deep, powerful feeling. Fear can be minimized by trusting you are exactly where you are supposed to be. Fear serves an important purpose in the process of taking flight. It gives you pause to check your flight plan and see if you are on course. This is when faith steps in to give you hope and courage to move beyond your fears.

What follows are stories that show how fear can stop you from following your dreams. The first one is from Ruthie.

My Box of Stories

One early October morning, I was busy fixing breakfast when the doorbell rang. I peered out the window to see who was there. I was puzzled. There wasn't anyone at the door. I know I was not imagining something. I heard the doorbell ring. I opened the door. There, on the front step, was a box. I picked it up and plunked the box onto the living room floor. There wasn't a return address.

That's strange, I thought. My curiosity was piqued. I tore the paper off the box and peered into it. Tears rolled down my cheeks. Inside was a box of stories. They were from Aunt Franny.

Aunt Franny had died several months earlier. I looked through the stories she had written. I thought of the West African folktale, Anansi the Spider. The Sky God had kept all the stories from the creatures in the world until Anansi struck a bargain. He hoped the Sky God would give him the stories of sadness, happiness, and the mysteries of the world. Anansi met the Sky God's demands. He was given the box of stories. Stories swirled in the air when he opened the box. Creatures jumped up, catching some of the stories before a big wind came along. The rest of the stories were carried to the four corners of the world.

Aunt Franny's stories were like that. They found their way to me. The stories contained the themes of the Sky God's stories. They were filled with happiness, sadness, and things she was never able to resolve. They were mysterious.

I have a vivid picture of Aunt Franny sitting at her vintage manual typewriter. Aunt Franny's dream was to become a published author. She told everyone in the family her dream. We believed her dream would eventually be realized.

Growing up, I listened to her stories many times. Aunt Franny's favorite phrase was, "If you have heard this, raise your hand." My cousins and I would raise our hands, and she would say, "Too bad. I must tell you this story one more time."

Looking back, I wonder if that was her way to ensure we would remember her. Today, I would give anything to have Aunt Franny tell me her stories one more time.

—Ruthie

My Shocking Diagnosis

Mitzi Dunford is a licensed clinical social worker. She lives in Salt Lake City, Utah, where she enjoys the beauty of the mountains and finds the ocean to be her power place. Mitzi shows up with a tapestry of vision and wisdom created from years of seeking to understand and apply universal truths to her immediate life and for the clients she works with daily. She participates in studies to understand and eliminate melanoma.

When asked what stopped her from pursuing her dreams, she said allowing herself to become distracted from her inner self was the main culprit. When you are focused on your true self, you can fully develop as a self-actualized individual, free to live your happiest possible life. Here's Mitzi's story.

Mitzi was hanging curtains in her guest bedroom when the phone rang. It was her doctor. He said, "You have melanoma." Weeks later, Mitzi came out of surgery with two large areas of skin, muscle, and melanoma taken from her leg. A deep, permanent wound was left behind. Six months passed. Mitzi was determined not to be defined by the cancer. She adamantly refused to wear a ribbon, hike for cancer, or participate in activities that labeled her "cancer victim." She wanted her old life back. She went to her guest room to find the curtains laying on the bed. Her world had stopped. Cancer interrupted her dreams.

Her career path stalled, instead, she focused on her physical health.

Mitzi fully recovered. She resumed her quest becoming a psychologist sitting with clients listening to their stories. Mitzi shared how honored she is by her client's trust. Mitzi says, "When my inner clock slows and time slows, it is a red flag for me to pay attention."

She has found turning around a command she often heard in childhood—"Don't just stand there. Do something!" to "Don't just do something. Stand there!"—creates calm.

There is joy in the sorrow and sorrow in the joy.
—Mitzi Dunford

Making the Goal

Tanner Antolak has a bachelor of science degree in entrepreneurship and innovation from Metropolitan State University in Minneapolis, Minnesota, and life coach practitioner certification from the International Center of Coaching, Learning Journeys. He is employed by the Big Know. His team creates brands and businesses development inspired education strategies. He dedicates his free time to playing ice hockey, starting new business ventures, and spending time with friends and family. Tanner lives in Minneapolis, Minnesota, with his girlfriend, Lila.

At the time of this writing, the COVID-19 pandemic was raging across the country. The virus interrupted the lives of virtually everyone on the planet, and Tanner's life was no exception. The virus made him question his path. Everything in his life and the lives of everyone around him swiftly diverted from familiar, friendly, and obvious to unknown, bizarre, and obscure because of COVID-19. He's been left with no clear signal how to obtain what he desires. Making laundry lists of to-dos attracts and burdens him. They shut him down. They stop him from trusting his process. Excuses overwhelm him diminishing taking action. Tanner had a breakthrough.

Hockey is Tanner's breakthrough. It gives him the energy to lock horns with issues he is brawling with. When all seems lost in life, hockey has had Tanner's back. When he thought all was lost, he got on the ice. It reminds Tanner that struggle can lead to strength. It told him if he was going to hell, just keep going. In Tanner's mind, hell was way too hot for him. When Tanner is wearing hockey skates, a mouth guard, a helmet, and full body protection, he believes his mind and thoughts are still vulnerable. The hockey stick leads him. Determination and commitment give him the goal. When he slams the puck into the net, he scores.

During the pandemic, Tanner's team has played hockey. Small changes have been implemented. Players must have their uniforms on prior to entering the building. Locker rooms are off-limits. Masks must be worn entering the building until game time. Family and friends can attend games. They must wear masks and social distance in the bleachers. The roar of the crowd is no longer a roar. It is muffled.

When Tanner has a unique idea filled with passion, he keeps going. He tries over and over again knowing, he can score his winning goal.

If you feel stuck, having an urge or itch, change course.
—Tanner Antolak

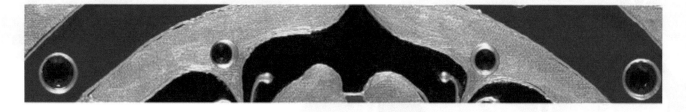

My Baby Wouldn't Stop Crying

Heidi Tuneberg is an advocate for people with disabilities. She is a certified change management leader. She is a certified Lean Six Sigma Yellow Belt methodology. Her career path includes vice president and director of project management, senior director, and Us Marketing Creative Operations+Studio for Best Buy. Heidi, her husband, Matt; and their two sons live in Woodbury, Minnesota.

Heidi's story involves her son, Jackson, and a situation no parent ever wants to be in. Here's her story in her own words:

The sound of Jackson crying could be heard throughout the house for the first two years of his life. Due to his heightened sensory situation, Jackson had a very discerning palette from the time he was born. As a baby, we exhausted every bottle, formula, and configuration humanly possible. His discernment earned trips to the doctor, and eventually, we found one formula he would eat (we called it liquid gold due to its cost as a specialty formula). As he grew, he ate something from every category of food, but his list of exceptions on *how* he'd eat them was extraordinary and fraught with rules. Medically, his growth-chart percentile registered him as the skinniest little guy for many years. Circle cheese from Cub Foods only, mac and cheese with I Can't Believe It's Not Butter (not real butter), Oscar Meyer hot dogs—no substitutes. The list was significant, and if he was served something, his sensory went into overload, and he could tell the difference between even the smallest of nuances (and not seeing how the food was prepared). Suffice it to say, we had many mac and cheese bowls shared back to me with a little smile, untouched, with a simple message, "I must have gotten a bad batch."

Jackson attended food school, a sensory therapy focused on all aspects of eating. The three-year therapy was outstanding, and we are proud parents of a child who dared to drink an Oreo shake at age ten, downed his first cheeseburger at age twelve, and eats circle, square, rectangle, and all sorts of cheeses today.

Due to his audible sensory sensitivities, we did not realize how challenging it was for Jackson to be in situations with a lot of noise. The noises we were hearing were excruciating to Jackson. We made adjustments to our routines, allowing headphones at the table for ambient noise, making sure we got a quiet table, and having the courage to leave when we knew there was a choice between battling the elements or having a peaceful meal. This same young man uses his learned skills today, with headphones in hand and a quiet exit plan in case it gets to be too much.

Jackson had an incredible fear for babies, who were, unfortunately, his proclaimed archnemesis. Babies were a culmination of all the really difficult things for him. They were loud, unpredictable, and in truth, often smelly. Where a baby existed, we could not. If they were crying on the other side of a grocery store, he could hear them, and it was as painful, as if they were wailing directly into his ears. In public, we'd scout diligently to find a place where a baby was not, and at dinners out, we'd pray a baby was not seated near us. If they were, we had to leave. This went on for years!

Today, he is still not 100 percent when it comes to trusting babies, he's come an incredibly long way. A sick baby recently vomited all over him from the seat behind him on an airplane. He managed through the tough situation and promptly asked me to book first-row exit seats whenever we fly.

Jackson's list goes on, but there's one thing it's taught us both: what you see and what is happening right in front of you is in the eye of the beholder. Two people can be in one place, hearing, seeing, and smelling all the same things yet have significantly different experiences. It's up to us to reject judgment, blanket statements, and words our parents taught us, like, "Oh, you're fine." It's incumbent upon us to approach others curiously, be open to how they experience life, and have an open mind to accept what we weren't taught.

As for how he's doing today? He's amazing, and he's still working harder than anyone in the room to do the things that may seem simple to others. But he's doing it! He's graduated high school, had his first job, is learning to drive, and is now a junior in college. We're still working on slowing down, listening, and having open minds—a lifelong journey for us all.

Heidi's tenacity and determination found solutions for Jackson's needs. Jackson's medical challenges have greatly improved because of his mother's perseverance. She found a way to make certain Jackson's care providers listened and responded. Heidi set aside her fear and listened to her inner voice to find answers and give her son the best opportunities for quality of life. She learned to flip her script when the medical team wasn't providing Jackson with tangible solutions.

Heidi believes desire is pivotal in achieving dreams. Her dream was for her son, Jackson. Heidi comes from the certainty that we are each in charge of our journey, every day. Heidi has learned how to pause, listen, and discern when she is unsure of her next step. Her goal is to leave our planet better than she found it. Each day, she asks herself, *What three things did I leave better today?* She believes luck is something you make.

I have never felt I never belonged. I believe I belong because I belong, because I am here. I have the right, the privilege, and the responsibility to belong to myself. This is all.
—Heidi Tuneberg

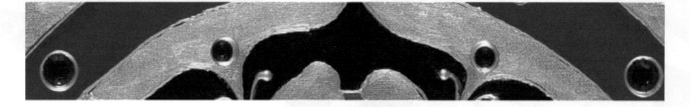

On the Other Side of My Trauma

Carolyn Chavez was born in Las Vegas, Nevada. She is a top-producing real estate agent, entrepreneur, wife, and owner of two dogs. She calls her girlfriends her soul sisters. She is a founder of Woman of Worth, for the entrepreneur. She is a founding member of the Mastermind Group, called Bad Ass Mastermind. She is the recipient of the first annual Salt Lake Board of Realtors Top Five Hundred Award. Carolyn lives in Salt Lake City, Utah.

When asked what kept her from achieving her dreams, she quickly pointed to her tendency to imagine herself as small or nearly invisible, a mere speck in the universe. Her feelings of discontentment persisted until she realized she was the biggest obstacle to getting the life she longed for. Here is her story:

Consider looking through the hauntings eyes of a young child who was exposed to poverty, chaos, mental illness, murder, sexual abuse, and substance abuse. This environment created a very shy and timid child. This is Carolyn, who saw herself as a fly on the wall imagining herself as invisible.

This quiet and watchful nature led Carolyn to graduate third in her high-school class, receiving a full-ride scholarship to the University of Nevada, Las Vegas. Carolyn worked in the restaurant industry with the goal of one day owning her own business. Terrified to speak to customers, she patterned herself after her boss, who would ask questions and develop relationships with the clientele. This experience taught her how to engage with people. Carolyn went on to become a Realtor and is a top-producing agent in her company.

Carolyn had a life-changing event when a friend gave her tickets to Tony Robbins's "Unleash the Power." Carolyn realized how her limiting beliefs were holding her back. She learned that the sky is the limit and that we have our own unique power beyond measure to become what we strive to be. Since this experience, Carolyn has been on a constant quest of self-development. Forward motion is key to realizing her dream. She quit her job and moved to Salt Lake City, Utah, to begin the process of becoming a realtor. This was a difficult choice, as in 2008, the real-estate market crashed in Utah.

Limiting beliefs, unhealthy learned behaviors, and perfectionism were the bullies paralyzing Carolyn. She learned from a mentor that progress itself is perfection. Every day, she practices results and how to navigate the minefield of rejection. She listens to podcasts taking massive action keeps her bullies at bay.

Learning to value herself is a great outcome for Carolyn. Engaging with people was the first step to creating relationships of trust. Closing a real estate transaction required getting out of her comfort zone. Carolyn came into the office early to rehearse scripts and learn how to ask questions of her clients that created objectivity and results. She learned that she could not control the market. She learned that she could control her mindset and attitude.

I belong in a bigger way
to a bigger world.
I still feel like the small fish
In the big pond.
I am Bold
I am Brave.
—Carolyn Chavez

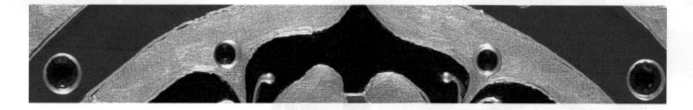

Great Questions to Ask

- Who gets in the way of soaring high?
- Who is your loudest voice supporting your dreams?
- What role does hope play?

_____

_____

_____

_____

_____

_____

_____

_____

_____

_____

_____

_____

_____

_____

_____

_____

Themes, Core Concepts, and Lessons Learned

- Fear is a powerful force.
- Minimize fear by trusting you are exactly where you're supposed to be.
- Fear gives us an important process for pause and course correction.

Chapter Notes and Resources

Typically, fear gets in our way from the start, or it can show up intermittently when we are on our dream flights. Research studies suggest that how you experience fear has to do with the content. When your thinking brain gives you feedback to your emotional brain and you decide you are still safe regardless of the situation in front of you, you can quickly shift the way you experience fear. Instead of allowing it to paralyze you, you can draw on a positive feeling, such as excitement.

Bakht, Arash Javan, and Saab, Linda. "What Happens in The Brain When we Feel Fear?" *Smithsonian Magazine*, October 20, 2017.

CHAPTER 4

What If Getting Lost Is Good?

I am always lost, I am found as well.
—Dave Powers

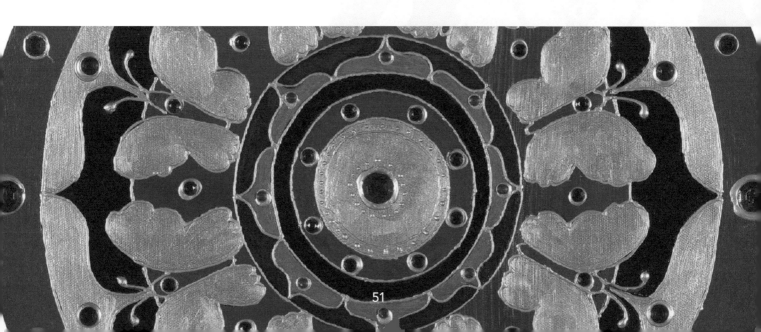

Mandala and The Butterfly

Experiencing a mandala can be like getting lost. Lost can be the best thing that ever happened. When you feel lost, what if you are being nudged to take a new direction and perspective? This gives you the opportunity to see your dreams in a new light.

For the butterfly, getting lost is not an option. For the Monarch butterfly, having a faulty internal compass guarantees an early death. However, what about the moment a caterpillar moves from a tree branch to a busy sidewalk? What about the selection of the caterpillar's resting place during its chrysalis stage? Scientific research has discovered that a caterpillar has an intrinsic knowing whereby their imaginal cells switch from programming themselves as a caterpillar to using a higher frequency of cells that cluster. Clustering cells begin the process of becoming a butterfly. You, too, have an intrinsic knowing to tap into and create your path. When has being lost transformed you?

How you choose to navigate and process your feelings of being lost can create a breakthrough or a breakdown. How can you give yourself permission to accept being lost as part of your many dream flights ? How can you believe you will find the direction of your dreams? How can being in the right place at the right time, though lost, turn into the best outcome imaginable? Here are some stories that answer these questions. The first one is from Ruthie.

My Space in Between

To me, destiny implies the experiences in my life are predetermined and shape my destiny. I do know choices present themselves along the way. Every moment, when I am standing at a choice point, I wonder should I go left, should I go right, or should I stay right where I am?

Many times, I have made the wrong decision, wondering, *How did I get here?* It is then that this inner voice manages to surface, shouting, "Well, my dear, you are the one who orchestrated this outcome." For example, there was the decision in college when I was determined to get a job at the Parks and Recreation department. The only problem with that idea was they had one opening, as an archery instructor. I told myself, *It can't possibly be that difficult.* It became that difficult when the interviewer asked me to demonstrate an archery lesson. I had no idea where to start. The interviewer looked me directly in my eyes and said, "You don't know one thing about archery, do you?"

Sheepishly, I said, "Not really."

I realized the choices I make are my responsibility. This doesn't necessarily mean I am responsible for everything that happens. I am responsible for the paths I take and the goals I set.

I always thought goals were a necessity to achieve what I desired. They led me to believe there must be a safe place to land. I told myself, *Keep your eye on the ball.* The message was repeated in the motivational books I read. The thought occurred to me: *What if they are wrong?* When I am constantly focused on my goal, what am I missing along the way? What am I not seeing that I might see? What am I not hearing that I might hear?

There must be someone to blame for the idea of goals. I decided to look up the culprit on the internet. Edwin A. Locke, a professor at the University of Maryland, was the initiator of goal-setting in the late 1960s. I wonder if he ever came to the same conclusion. Probably not.

Today, I find setting intentions to be more satisfying. Intentions allow me to imagine a destiny without attachment to the outcome. I can visualize and hold a picture in my mind of how I want to feel. God will nudge me toward the next right dream for me. I will just know.

When I think about the journey of dreams, I want it to be long—filled with warm summer days, delightful surprises, and thrilling adventures, just like in Cavafy's poem "Ithaca." His wish is that our journey will be "full of adventures and passions that stir our mind, body, and spirit." He reminds us not to fear the monsters of old. "You will not encounter fearful monsters if you do not carry them within your soul, if your soul does not set them up in front of you." He is telling us to let go of our old wounds and our past hurts. When we do, we will have an extraordinary journey, filled with joy. We will reach our destination full of awakenings.

Today, my journey is in what I would call the space in between. I have left the known, yet I have not quite stepped into the unknown, over the threshold, into my waking dreams. Recently, my daughter and I moved our business to another city. Before that, our business was at my home. When we moved the business, we decided to buy all new furniture. Consequently, we left all the old furniture at my house.

I had never really thought about how the move would affect me internally. We had thought that instead of moving all at once, we would get the business infrastructure up and running in our new location. I would then decide to move or to stay in my home. It sounded logical. We were taking one step at a time. However, I don't know what I was thinking. Logic never seems to work for me. I feel as if I am left with the books and paintings. It feels as if the energy of the people who entered my home is still here. It is as though each person left unfinished sentences on the floor and I am left to pick them up. There is an inescapable, daunting feeling of stillness that lingers in the air. I know intellectually that it is in the silent knowledge something new will emerge. I know God often speaks to me in my stillness. I find I am impatient, waiting for a sign to guide me. How can I untangle who I was in the past and define who I am today?

What is this space in between? It is the space where my inner knowing is recognized. The in-between space offers me time to reflect on what I no longer need. It is a time of releasing aspects of my past and embracing possibilities in my future.

—Ruthie

I Took a Perilous Risk

LiaMarie Applegarth grew up on the coast of Central California. After graduating from college, she took a job in Utah at Snowbird Ski and Summer Resort. This experience sparked her love of mountain living, backcountry skiing, climbing, and snowboarding. These sports added a new passion, and with it came mountain climbing. LiaMarie's move to the Wasatch, a mountain range in the western USA, led to her love for slot canyon exploration. LiaMarie has a Bachelors Degree from California Polytechnic State University, San Luis Obispo. She is currently enrolled in nursing school on her path to becoming a nurse anesthetist. She lives in Driggs, Idaho.

In this story, we join LiaMarie on an adventurous climb up the 11,326-foot Pfeifferhorn, deep in the heart of the Lone Peak Wilderness Area, in the Wasatch Mountains of Northern Utah. The climb is rated as difficult, reflecting its nickname—the Little Matterhorn. She tells her story in her own words.

> It was a day that started in the dark. Getting sandwiches and packs ready, I double- and triple checked my pack for my crampons, ice axe, and avalanche gear. We moved quietly along in the early morning darkness. The four of us moved in unison on skis and split boards, with special climbing skins attached to keep us from sliding backward on our ascent. We paced ourselves to conserve energy for a the most difficult part of the climb. The plan was to summit the 11,326-foot Pfeifferhorn, and ride the NW Couloir, a 50-degree couloir with a 40 foot rappel in the middle.

They climbed 2,440 vertical feet from their 7,660-elevation trailhead. They were moving in full view of the pronounced grandeur and difficulty of the Pfeifferhorn's final ascent. It was riddled with extreme exposure and severe consequences if mistakes were made. Their team of four became two. Their teammate decided to check out of the equation. He turned back to the trailhead to protect his safety with his teammate. LiaMarie and her teammate continued their climb reaching the summit.

The rappel chains and natural anchors they planned to use were buried under ice and snow. A patch of snow to the right of the entrance had a promising look and appeared to be a safe entrance into the couloir as the main entrance was all but impassable for a snowboard. Walking over rocks and maneuvering their way to the entrance, LiaMarie could feel the rigidity of the snow. It felt hard, but nothing that could not be ridden with skill and an ice axe could not bite into. She slowly descended. It became clear that what had seemed manageable was not. The route steepened beyond what was visible from above. The snow hardened making it impossible for her snowboard to keep an edge. At the same time, her teammate who was taking the main entrance made it only a few feet through a steep and rocky entrance before a rock knocked one of his skis off. It came to rest 30 feet below, just above the rappelling section. This was not the plan her team leader had laid out. She lowered her board a foot at a time, followed by her upper body. She reset her ice axe with each descent kicking her board against the hard surface to get a solid hold. The slope dropped off to a perilous degree of steepness. Every move threatened to send her free-falling and spinning out of control. Suddenly, LiaMarie found herself sliding uncontrollably down the steepening slope unable to get her ice axe into the hard surface. Another attempt, LiaMarie dug her ice axe into the hard surface. She came to a terrifying halt. She had slid twenty to thirty feet through the steepest portion of the couloir.

She couldn't catch her breath and calm her racing heart. She was afraid to move. Her ice axe was her lifeline.

Luckily for LiaMarie, her partner had recovered his lost ski and was able to climb up to her, replace her snowboard with crampons to help her safely make her way down to the rappel. What followed was a successful rappel, ride of the apron below, and navigation back to the road, passing iconic lines on her bucket list. Late season conditions led to lots of traversing and navigation through bare patches and waterfalls on the adventure out. Meanwhile, great lessons had been learned. Getting up is only the beginning. When taking risks, it does not do to ignore one set of conditions when all else seems perfect. Lastly, the allure of an easy entrance is a dangerous trap. This particular route was discussed a few days later with a friend who had also succumbed to this appealing entrance only the day before.

"If you're going to test your limits in the mountains, make sure there's not a 40 foot cliff below you."
—LiaMarie Applegarth

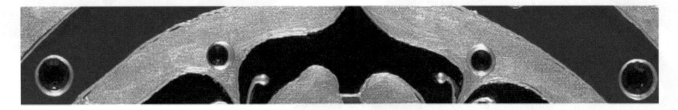

The Scream I Heard

Zoë Robbins was raised by free-spirited and adventurous parents, who live in Colorado and Maui. Zoë was drawn to the steep mountains and deep snow of Utah. She attended nursing school at Westminister College, Sugarhouse, Utah, where she discovered her passion for mental-health nursing. She became a psychiatric nurse practitioner and steward of her community mental health system. RN, DNP, PMH-NP University of Utah. She highly values and maintains a balance between hard work, adventure, and mothering her beloved daughter. Zoë is inspired by literature, film, and the true-life stories of tragedy and triumph entrusted to her through her work. Weekends are for enjoying friends and family. Snowboarding in the winter, followed by bicycling, boating, and going to yard sales in the summer are her enjoyments. Travel is the cherry on her sundae of life, and she dreams of one day traveling—not for vacation but as a mission with a specific purpose. Zoë lives in Salt Lake City, Utah. When she's lost, she takes time to heal, reflect, and choose. This created resilience in her; she had to learn how to accept the challenges life threw at her.

Here is her story.

How could the ocean be pulling back from the shoreline like that, sucking itself in, revealing reefs, fish, and large fishing boats, which were instantly destroyed by the tsunami, which was moving at least five hundred miles per hour? This is what happened on December 26, 2004, when a 9.4 earthquake struck in the Indian Ocean. The earthquake and tsunamis took the lives of 230,000 people in fourteen countries.

Five weeks later, Zoë found herself in the throes of pain and suffering, horror and hope, loss and love. She went to Sri Lanka to contribute her skills to heal and help one person at a time wherever relief was requested by Medicines Global (GB) for survivors.

It would take Zoë many years as a psychiatric nurse practitioner to realize she had not chosen the profession simply because she was fascinated by the human mind. Her relationship with mental health and wellness started when she was about eight years old.

She thinks of the pitch of her mother's scream as she learned from the person on the other line of the phone that her grandfather had committed suicide by gun—as many men in his family had before him.

Over the next fifteen years, Zoë lost a disproportionate number of her teenage friends to suicide, overdose, drunk driving, avalanches, and murder.

She was fascinated and frightened by the story of her mom's sister having a psychotic break at a hunting lodge deep in the woods of British Colombia. The weird, wobbly, and wonderful experiences her mother's own mood swings brought to her childhood are now equal parts historical clinical observation and painful recollection.

Zoë is the one person in her nursing school's graduating class to focus on mental health. She returned to school for a master in psychiatric nursing before the year was out. She said she began to realize human instinct causes us to reflect on our traumas.

Zoë feels at home when she patiently moves through a crisis with a client or keeps pace with a person in the throes of mania. In graduate school, she was assigned to facilitate a grieving group, progressing into volunteer work for several years.

She said, "I was healing my own grief through the stories and emotions of others." Zoë posed the question, "Who is healing who?" Her career has been her most effective defense mechanism and source of healing.

Zoë's mantra is, "Hang in there." Today, she has become Dr. Zoë Robbins. Dr. Robbins has pursued her doctorate in psychology and attained her PhD.

Fear,
I know how to deal with you.
There is no going under,
Over or around
Only through you.
Descending into your belly,
I have the power to pull the curtains back.
I am surprised
A flood of light appears.
It washes a new color over me.
I am no longer frightened
By you.
I move in and out
Of intense spaces.
Vulnerable to the wisps of air,
I sit, I trust, I hold space,
My pain washes over me
I emerge.
—Zoë Robbins

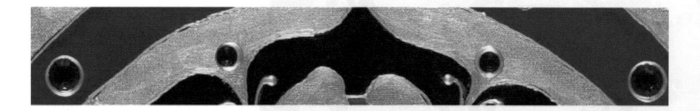

Great Questions to Ask

- When have you felt lost?
- How did it affect you?
- How did you find your way?

_____

_____

_____

_____

_____

_____

_____

_____

_____

_____

_____

_____

_____

_____

_____

_____

Themes, Core Concepts, and Lessons Learned

- Being lost is a part of our *dream flight*.
- How we process being lost determines our outcome.
- You must choose to believe you're in the right place at the right time.

Chapter Notes and Resources

Feeling lost is a sign you're becoming more present in your life—you're living less within the narratives and ideas that are premeditated and more in the moment at hand.

—Harley Diala, "For When You Feel Lost in Life," *Thought Catalog*

CHAPTER 5

Who Is Most Likely to Soar with You?

Anyone who is a supporter surprises me. It is a selfless act.
—Jennie Antolak

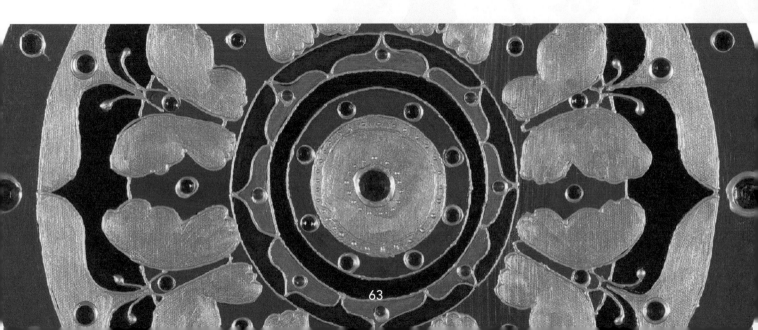

63

Mandala and The Butterfly

The mandala is a portal to motivation in action. The mandala has a request: "Please peer into my center and allow yourself to soar." Mandalas are designed with a pattern reflecting the highest good and the deepest part of your soul. The mystery radiates. You can soar beyond the unexpected when you see a mandala. You can let go of the ego "brain" and move into your "heart" knowing. You can release your sense of control and expectations. The nourishing nectar of the flowers soars with the butterfly. Your inner knowing and connection with people is your nourishment.

When you recognize your soul, the essence of who you are, it becomes your constant companion in flight. Your soul is an unknown mystery of life that is yours to embrace and lean on. Your soul does not live in a vacuum; like your body, it requires sustenance. Sustenance comes from self-love and the love of those around you.

What happens when you disregard the support that stands in the wings? The answer to this question is easy. Weathering a storm alone is much more difficult than weathering it with two. At times, we resist others soaring with us while we strive to achieve our dreams. There is strength in numbers. Keeping an open heart will help you spot the people who can best support you on your flight path. We trust the following stories will inspire you to reach out for the love and support already existing in your world. Look around to see where the source of your positive energy lives. Grab it, claim it, name it, express it, and don't let go! The first story is from Ginnymarie.

Who Gave Me This Gift?

Magical, free movement is the way I describe how I feel when I am ice-skating. My earliest memory is me, clinging to a wooden rocking horse my father whipped in circles across the ice skating rink. My father towed me across the ice with strength and certainty, or was that my view through four-year-old eyes? I loved the strength, power, and sheer joy of soaring across the ice. It was like indelible ink imprinting a deep desire in me to experience this again and again.

"Can I take ice skating lessons?" became my daily mantra from the age of three. The answer was always the same: "No!"

One day, yes happened. I took lessons at the winter outdoor rink. I never found out who my benefactor was. At the age of ninety-two, my mother continued to keep this secret from me. I wanted to know who it was. I wanted to thank them.

Something happened that I will never know. Soon, I was taking two to four private indoor ice-skating lessons a week and skating thirty hours. Lessons were sixty dollars an hour. This was the early 1960s. My mother would wake me at 4:15 a.m. to drive to the ice center. I began my day with an hour of what was called "patch." This was the practice of making perfect figure eights and small loops with a precise diameter. This requires every muscle to be in control. The goal is to achieve a figure eight three times without touching the ice with both skates while creating the diagram. Freestyle lessons followed. My pro, Dick Vraa, taught me how to do single and double jumps. Triples and quads had not been invented yet. I loved jumping in the air, feeling such magical free movement. It was a feeling of freedom as, in that millisecond in time, I felt my being and not my physical self.

Each time I fell and got up to try again, I came one step closer to success. Within three months, I mastered all freestyle double jumps and was working on the flying camel and flying sit spins. I was an innocent, living in the moment, happy, and unaffected child. September was approaching, signaling there would be national-level judges testing skaters for their school figures and freestyle abilities at our rink.

My pro decided it was time to take my first several tests. This process was required to test to the gold level for qualification to regional, national, and international competitions and the Olympic trials. I was not afraid. The day of the test, I put on the soft white, pink, and blue skating dress my mother sewed for me. I weighed sixty pounds, petite and small for my age. The judges nodded for me to skate to the designated area. Upon finishing, I sat in the bleachers, waiting to hear if I had passed.

The announcement never came. There was a big disappointment. Only one person had passed. She was not a member of the local ice-skating club. She was not rich and did not have parents watching her skate every morning wearing a mink coat or three-piece suit. She was not part of the skating community at the economic level.

That girl was me. The judges, the rink manager, and my pro told me not to share my success. I was ten years old. This was a big embarrassment for the club. I did not understand what had happened. All I knew was I had accomplished something very special.

Even today, I am puzzled as to how this event marked the end of my dream to have a competitive skating career. Without knowing it, I learned that my parents' "yes" gave me an experience that created a courageous outlook in me. This experience shaped my future self. It taught me that the people who I admired were weak, fearful, and unsure of themselves. As a child, I never understood what had happened.

I went on to teach skating to fund my college education. I have my benefactor and mother to thank.

At the age of forty, I decided to pursue ice-dancing. With aching feet and the courage to work through my fears, I learned to dance with a loving double-gold-medalist ice-dancer and freestyle coach. That summer, a dream was realized.

Soaring across the ice with my skating partner, we passed the first three national-level ice-dancing tests. The excitement, pressure, and thrill of being one with the music and one with my partner awakened my soul.

Unlike my experience three decades ago, there was clapping in the audience and announcements from the loudspeaker. My husband of twenty years was standing in the bleechers, clapping for me.

—Ginnymarie

I am filled with wonder
Realizing
Who is
Soaring alongside me.
—Ginnymarie Leines and Ruth M. Godfrey

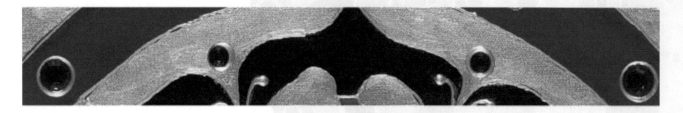

My Unusual Partner

Denielle Jones tried horseback riding after a long struggle with drug addiction. She developed a passion, changing her life. After many years of getting to the barn at six in the morning, practicing and working with her horse, Denielle won the Arabian Horse Association National Championship. Denielle's husband, Mike, assisted her at competitions, helped with creating her hair salons, and navigated the journey of their blended family. She is the epitome of grit. Denielle raised four children as a single mother, until 1999.

Denielle's life has not always been like that. She had been at the mercy of methamphetamine addiction. She tried to take her own life by overdosing on methamphetamines and alcohol in 1999. Her youngest child, who was eight years old (her siblings were ten, eleven, and twelve at the time), found her mother lying on the floor. She couldn't tell if she was dead or alive. She dialed 911. Denielle's life was saved by her eight-year-old daughter. The police, fire department, and later that day, social services came to her home. The children were taken into protective custody.

Once she was medically evaluated, Denielle was transported to a rehab facility attached to the county jail. She had no one to turn to for help. There were no relatives living nearby. The children were put in foster care. For thirty days, they were without their mother while she went through detoxification. The following month, she returned home.

Denielle had strict supervision, attending Narcotics Anonymous six times a week. The children were allowed to move back home. The county provided counseling and resources to help Denielle with her family. She met a gentleman named Mike at a Narcotics Anonymous meeting. He became her close friend, and soon, he was becoming part of her family and her future husband.

When the children were older, Mike recognized that Denielle didn't have personal passions. He suggested she try horseback riding.

Denielle's years of hard times and seeking sobriety created self-discipline and focus. These identical traits translated into national award-winning horsemanship, horse performances, and successful entrepreneurship.

We were unbeatable because of the great love relationship we had.
—Denielle Jones

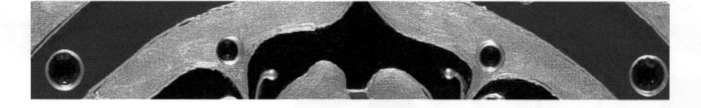

My Tipping Point

Tim Boyle grew up in the northeastern United States. His passion for skiing started at Sugarbush, Vermont, at age six. He went on to become a member of the ski team at Lawrenceville School in the early 1980s. Tim moved to Salt Lake City, Utah, soon thereafter to become a ski bum at Snowbird Ski Resort. In 1997, he began a daily meditation practice, tai chi, with the aid of Michael Brown's Presence Practice. He holds a Bachelors of Art and Philosophy, *maxima cum laude,* from LaSalle University. Skiing a steep powder line in the winter, mountain biking in the summer, and attending the symphony are his passions. Tim lives in Huntsville, Utah.

Tim is a seeker of enlightenment. He meditates daily, is an avid reader, and studies philosophers and statesmen. His recognition and insight for the basis of his transformation is set forth in his statement of gratitude for all the dreamers who have blazed a trail to self-discovery, leading to Tim's own personal growth. Here is his statement, in his own words.

> The dreamers I cherish and admire are the writers, artists, composers, philosophers, saints, and mystics, as well as the Son of God and Buddha. They are the people from out of time, the authors of every book I have read, the ideas snatched from other minds in their myriad rays of light hitting old velum or wood pulp, etched into eternity and showered down on the piece of light I am, here now, in this moment. These are the surprising people who have helped me, sustained me, encouraged me, and fed me, mentally and spiritually. I wish I knew them better. To know them at all is enough. Then it is one's family, friends, and strangers— one and all, who allow me to see into myself through an entirely enhanced prism.

Tim believes through mindfulness practices, combined with gratitude, he becomes who he is called to be. Tim practices meditation daily, continues to read and reread the great philosophers of all time for insight and guidance. He spends time in nature to maintain gratitude in the moment. Tim believes each of us has the power of choice. We can embrace our awakening dreams with the thoughts, minds, and majesty of the tipping-point encounters we've had through our life experiences.

Time recognizes we can reflect and consider where the writers, artists, philosophers, God, and more sit with us. We can choose to soar with them, in the space in between spaces. This creates a new perspective of what and who our greatest supporters are and can be.

What is Fascinating
is the Multitude of
Souls who have Ridden Along,
Side by Side with Me,
on My many Quests.
They are the People
From out of Time
Beyond and Within
—Tim Boyle

Great Questions to Ask

- Who is most likely to soar with you?
- How are they showing up in your life?
- How have they surprised you?

_____

_____

_____

_____

_____

_____

_____

_____

_____

_____

_____

_____

_____

_____

_____

_____

Theme, Core Concepts, and Lessons Learned

- It will surprise you who shows up to support you.
- People want to support your dreams.
- Disregarding support diminishes the opportunity for your dreams to flourish.

Chapter Notes and Resources

In the article "Surrounding Yourself with the Right People Changes Everything," Jennifer Cohen provides solid tips for choosing the right people:

- Say goodbye to the negative nellies in your life.
- Choose friends who are smarter than you.
- Cultivate real-life relationships with people who have accomplished your goals.
- Find alternative ways to be with like-minded people who have what you want. Study their media and imagine them as your friend. If you can't play tennis, watch the game, listen to their podcasts, and soak up their tips, tricks, and knowledge.

Cohen, Jennifer. "Surrounding Yourself with the Right People Changes Everything." *Forbes Magazine*, December 4, 2018.

CHAPTER 6

What about the Unexpected?

Dreams are my waking gift.
They show up unexpectedly.
Thank you.
—Ginnymarie M. Leines

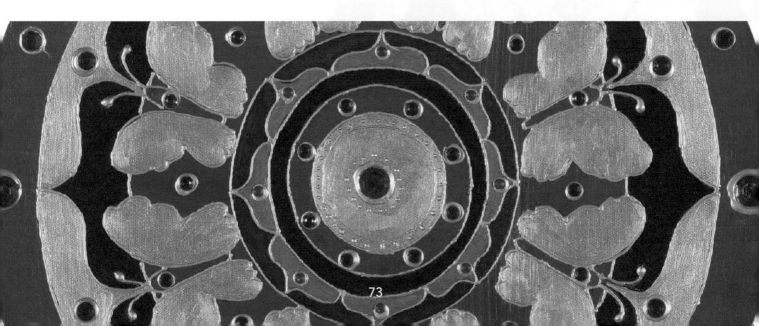

Mandala and The Butterfly

The mandala's power to fascinate you through the ages is a mystery that clouds objectivity. You continue to be drawn to something beyond your understanding. Being prepared and ready for the unexpected calls you to step back and become an observer of self.

   Butterflies aren't concerned with delayed, rerouted, or detoured flight plans. Their existence is spent landing on flowers attracting them to nourish and give them strength. The butterfly, in its pure innocence, proceeds through the birthing of itself as a caterpillar, the acceptance of becoming a chrysalis, to the strength it takes to move out into the world to spread its wings. You can mirror your dream flights after the butterfly and breathe with the wisdom of the mandala.

Surprise is your unexpected and constant companion in life. It's important to be prepared every day. How willing are you to be surprised? Delays, rerouting, and the unexpected are parts of flight you experience. The benefit allows you to recalculate and change course as needed. It may stretch you and challenge you, giving you deeper insights and understanding. Today, it's calling you to alter your course. It creates a time for reflection, a time to consider what is important, and a time to validate your dreams. Change is the circle of life. It often comes about when we least expect it. The following stories reflect how difficult it can be to accept change when it comes, whether we want it or not. This first story is from Ginnymarie.

My Uninvited Disease

My outlook on life lands me in places with positive results. This is a matter of opinion. We all get to have our own. I look for synergy in delays with unexpected route changes. I believe my invited guest created something bigger and better for my path.

Hope, is my conscious practice giving me inner knowing to trust wherever I am, the outcome is in my highest good. I learned to embrace the values I taught our sons, reminding myself who I am is how I live.

In the 1980s, our family lived on a thousand acres of wilderness—white and red oak forests, low-lying swamp, grassy meadows, and farm fields undulated alongside a sleepy river. We lived in the middle of a natural wildlife sanctuary, with beavers, foxes, eagles, and the occasional black bear and badgers. I wasn't aware of that we were living amongst a fast-growing population of Lyme-disease-infested wood ticks.

Wood ticks are prevalent in Minnesota. We accept them as a nuisance yet not a serious threat to our health. In summer, our family floated the river. We cut a twenty-mile single-track trail, taking us into the deepest woods, across meadows, and over fallen trees used as bridges, riding our mountain and dirt bikes.

One day, I saw a bright red bull's-eye on my calf muscle. I thought it was a spider bite. Several days later, I woke in the middle of the night. My kidneys were recoiling in pain. I felt nauseated. Painful malaise washed over my entire body. I waited for what seemed like an eternity. I called the nearest hospital to speak to an emergency-room nurse. She said I should come in. I waited. I felt better by morning. I wrote it off as the flu, food poisoning, or a spider bite. The bull's-eye went away. I never went to the hospital.

Two years went by. It was winter. I stood in the Snowbird Ski Resort tram line, waiting to go up the mountain to ski. Everything seemed to be going well. It was not. Suddenly, I felt as if I was going to pass out. My thought was, *Please, carry me away on a stretcher*. I felt weak, nauseated, and listless. The food I ate for breakfast had given me flu symptoms—or had it? The feeling passed. I pushed forward, put aside my thoughts, and rode the mountain with my family.

My winter continued, with episodes developing into a pattern of sudden sickness. Spring came, and I trained for a multiple sclerosis 150-mile bicycle ride fundraiser. My training partner and I did four days of 10-to-20-mile rides, and a 75-plus-mile ride every week. We were excited for our first MS 150. Mornings started with a 5:30 step class or weightlifting before work. I signed up to go on a five-day 500-mile bicycle trip to the north rim of the Grand Canyon. My cycling group managed a 17–19 average miles per hour, which was commendable considering we were riding up to 13-degree grades. The 49-mile push across the desert looked flat when, in fact, it was an uphill grade. I was elated with the feeling of moving together with a team of riders. Our motto was, "There are no heroes," we each rode for two minutes at the head of our pace line to capture optimum speed and conserve energy. This was our longest day of riding, completing 148 miles.

By all outward appearances, I was in top physical shape. This was not true at all. The Lyme disease was taking up residency in my body. I noticed sitting with my legs crossed had become very painful. I had to manually lift one leg off the other. Sitting in a yoga class with legs folded over each other was not an option. My joints ached. I saved myself from falling downstairs as my ankle or hip would lock up. Something was wrong.

I got back into my routine of aerobics and step class, along with weightlifting. My job was demanding. Overseeing and implementing business for two hundred employees working across seventeen states was very demanding. Luckily for me, I had documented and updated every phone call, task, daily, and weekly plan . My short-term memory was disappearing. While I was doing research at the library, I realized I had multiple symptoms of Lyme disease. I felt alone.

I began the quest for answers. My general practitioner assured me I did not have Lyme disease. I asked if I could be tested. She answered with a firm no. Instead, she recommended to get my thyroid and hormones tested. I sought out an integrative doctor. She found my thyroid was greatly compromised. My hormones checked out in the normal range. Again, I was told "no" when I asked if I could get a Lyme test. Both physicians denied my request for a test as Lyme disease was not recognized by insurance companies and testing models were not perfect. I instinctively knew I had Lyme disease. I found another doctor to speak with who recognized my short-term memory problems were becoming unmanageable. The doctor asked me to go in for a spinal tap and brain scan to determine if I had multiple sclerosis. I refused. I was beyond disappointed. He, too, refused to give me a Lyme test. I did not buy into his viewpoint. I kept this information to myself.

I made an appointment with the integrative medicine physician. Once again, I asked, "Please order a Lyme test for me." This physician wanted to deny my request as well. She saw my distress and agreed to order the test.

A week later, I received a call. The antibody blood test produced a prognosis of advanced Lyme-disease. The next day, I saw an epidemiologist, a well-known Lyme specialist. He spoke before Congress about Lyme disease. He was involved in creating awareness nationally and giving people the best immediate care. I felt relieved, hopeful, and exhausted. My energy level was low, and my faith in medicine had disappeared.

At the appointment, I was greeted with, "Dear, you have every symptom of Lyme's disease." Finally, I had landed where I needed to be. Two days later, I received a peripherally-inserted catheter in my left arm. I learned how to hook myself up to an antibiotic three times a day and flush the line to prevent blood clots. A home health nurse came to test my kidney and liver function twice a week to monitor organ distress. I looked at the PICC-Line as a small nuisance. My plan was to continue working, go to the gym every day, and get well. The gym idea collapsed on the first day. My PICC-Line backed up while I was holding my arm steady against my body doing step aerobics.

Weeks passed. Crazy though it may seem, I celebrated when I felt sick. Feeling sick meant the Lyme bacteria were dying off. They were seeking refuge where none existed. This reaction is called Jarisch-Herxheimer to endotoxin, byproducts released by the death of harmful microorganisms. After two months, my treatment concluded.

I felt exhausted. My foggy brain incidences had lessened, my knees no longer hurt, and my overall malaise and fatigue passed. I was proud how I didn't give up on what I found I had but didn't want. I refused to wallow in my problem. I lived with it as a force to be eradicated.

I have my integrative physician to thank for validating my request. I am grateful for the epidemiologist who cared for me. His research continues to find answers to eliminate the Lyme tick altogether.

My memory of Lyme disease anguish is stored away. Today, I continue to drop things, and I have painful skin neuropathy, a nonfunctional thyroid, and leg joints mysteriously locking when climbing stairs.

—Ginnymarie

Waking Up My Consciousness

Iliana Ivana is a graduate of the Preparatory Law School of Belgrade, Serbia. She is founder of the Toronto (Canada)-based FIG Social Group offering singles events for professionals. She calls herself an emotional healing coach. Her favorite saying is, "Everything is possible if you choose to believe." Here is her story.

Imagine for a moment that your cell phone pings—you have another email. It could be another bit of spam, or it could be an invitation beyond your wildest dreams. This is what happened to Iliana when she was invited to Dubai, United Arab Emirates. She brought her intuitive and healing gifts to her evolving friendships in the UAE, and together, they explored healing and spirituality. Iliana shared how she embraces faith and expresses gratitude. Iliana's gratitude journal creates continued balance in her world. Visualizing how she feels and what she desires is her daily practice.

Iliana posts on Facebook, runs social media sites, and frequently offers a podcast. She is well known for her podcast "Let Go and Let God." She provides workshops on developing your intuition. Her ongoing mission is to provide a platform for encouragement and hope to people experiencing hardships and conflict. She is intentionally transparent, sharing with her audiences her human frailty. Iliana's mission is to live in a state of *theta*. This is a state of mind where an individual is in his or her highest state of waking consciousness and meditation. She has been sharing her gifts of healing and spiritual mentorship for twenty years. Iliana would love to invite every living being to be a *spiritual badass*. This is someone who sends love out to strangers, seeks out lessons, and knows that happiness is a choice.

Life difficulties are course corrections to perfect our path.
—Iliana Ivana

I Was There in 1929

Jimmy Smith believes in the power of prayer. He prays daily and humbly on his knees in appreciation for the life he is living. "Today, at ninety," he says, "is just the beginning. I have a lot to want to stick around for."

Jimmy draws on Ghandi's quote: "Every man wants to live, every man wants to love, every man wants to learn, and every man wants to leave a legacy." Today, Jimmy has realized this quest, in part by becoming an internationally acclaimed motivational speaker who lectures on how to be a successful global direct sales marketer. He has six adult children, twenty-eight grandchildren, and thirty-two great-grandchildren. Today, he is a multimillionaire. Jimmy "The Butcher" Smith lives in Pennsylvania.

Jimmy's story shows you hard times can inspire big dreams.

"Your money is not safe. Banks closing."

It was 1929. Jimmy's family owned several butcher shops. Within a few months, their butcher shops were closed. They lost everything, and their butcher shops were boarded shut. Jimmy's father found himself and his extended family broke, with nothing. They knew people would need their butcher skills, eventually, they were able to find work. Jimmy and his family survived the Great Depression. It left an indelible mark, a tattoo never to lose its meaning, a message that whatever you do, make sure it's something people need. Jimmy's father's advice was to become a butcher, putting food on the table for his family. For forty years, Jimmy followed in his father's footsteps as a butcher. Their only concern was feeding their family, heating their home, and being together.

Jimmy injured his back and developed debilitating arthritis. He could no longer support his family as a butcher. For five years Jimmy searched for a new way to support his family. Jimmy became an expert at analyzing compensation plans and successfully monetizing a business. Jimmy became a millionaire in his new business enterprise by the time he reached the age of sixty-four. He developed a deep-seated belief growing up during the depression years: get a job regardless of what it is. This acknowledges the immediate needs of the family, providing basic human necessities, including food and shelter. His dream for his children was that they would all have a job. Jimmy realized this dream beyond his expectations. He mentored and advised his children who participated in his business.

Jimmy is the survivor of an unexpected physical collapse from acute spinal arthritis. He came back from bankruptcy in his early sixties to create a new job and legacy for his family. He patterned himself after core values he learned in childhood. His father had a sign in the butcher shop: "We cannot afford to have even one dissatisfied customer." Jimmy has exhibited this belief in his private and business life. He said being in service of others assures his success.

Don't look down on anyone except to pull them up. It is the law of reciprocity. The more you give, the more you receive.
—Jimmy Smith

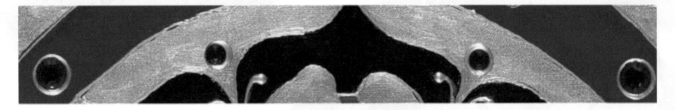

Great Questions to Ask

- How do you respond to delays, reroutings, and the unexpected?
- What are you encountering?
- What are these experiences giving you?

_____

_____

_____

_____

_____

_____

_____

_____

_____

_____

_____

_____

_____

_____

_____

_____

Themes, Core Concepts, and Lessons Learned

- Surprise is your unexpected and constant companion in life.
- Be prepared and ready for the unexpected.
- Be willing to be surprised.

Chapter Notes and Resources

People often give up when the unexpected happens. "Giving up is the most common form of failure," says Deep Patel, VIP Contributor. Mastering resilience is the key to realizing our dreams, success as we envision it, and staying on course when faced with the unexpected.

Patel, Deep. "Eight Ways Successful People Master Resilience." *Entrepreneur Magazine*, July 16, 2018.

CHAPTER 7

Who Are the Bullies Blocking Your Flight?

Doubts
and Misgivings
are
My Bullies.
—Carol Ann Docken Fisher

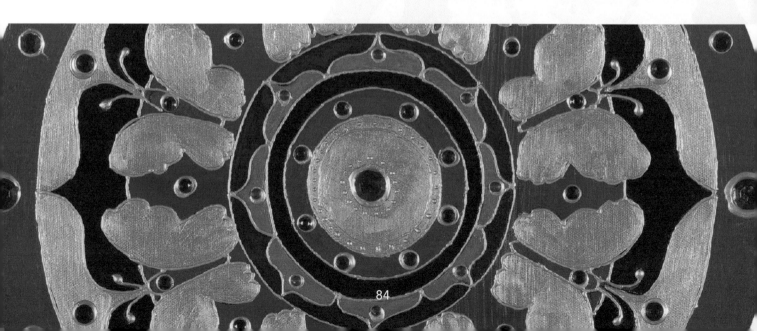

84

Mandala and The Butterfly

Once again, the mandala has a message for you: "Dear ones, please shed your ego, the beautiful, intellectual objective mind of yours, and imagine or gaze at me with wonder. How I wish to give you the gift you carry, a present to be opened with ease by moving from your head into your heart."

Many butterflies never make it to the chrysalis stage. Pelting rain and strong shoes squash their caterpillar selves walking on the pavement they chose to share with humans. An unsuspecting crow looking for a snack can end their beautiful transformation in a millisecond. Your inner voice can bully you into eroding your confidence and diminishing your focus.

Know your bullies. They can show up as guardians disguised as sheep, when in fact, they are waitng to strike. They are like a snake that recoils and bites. Their subconscious intention is to protect their insecurities. You can choose to dismiss the comments of bullies. You can choose to celebrate your movement toward your dreams.

It's critically important to surround yourself with a community of people who champion you. Negative people create negative effects in your lives. Befriend people who want positive action in their lives. Equally important is to separate yourself from people who pull you down. When you are around negative people, your beliefs can be undermined and you can be robbed of intrinsic hope.

As you experience your dream flights; realize negative people in your life will try to tear you down. Walk away. Seek the positive. Bullies are a fact of life. Here are some stories that may help you understand how to deal with bullies.

My Father's Stand

Christina Arnold is a dedicated attorney. In her spare time, she loves to read, and she is an accomplished singer. When a travel adventure presents itself, she packs her bags. Christina lives in Willisau, Canton of Luzern, Switzerland.

Christina struggled with school and believed she was not a good student. "I almost flunked out of school. One year before I was to leave for America as an exchange student, my father received a call from one of my teachers.

"My teacher told my father, 'If this were my child, I would not let her leave. She will come back screwed up for life. She will be lost.'"

Christina's father didn't listen to the teacher's advice. He firmly believed if he let Christina go, she would not finish school and he would lose her as well.

Christina fulfilled her desire to be an exchange student in 2009. When she arrived in the States she spoke very little English. Originally, Christina was drawn to the US because of what she saw in the movies. Reality hit her when she arrived in Minneapolis, Minnesota. The day of her arrival, Minneapolis was hit by a tornado. Lightning, thunder, and tornado-warning sirens were new to Christina. Now, at three in the morning, some crazy American was screaming to take cover. Christina wasn't sure what she was being told. She now knew that hearing the language was not the same as watching a movie in her Swizz town of Willisau. Within a year, she came to understand all the terms related to severe Minnesota storms and mastered English in other areas as well.

She was chosen to be the lead in the high school play, which required speaking, singing, and dancing. She mastered all three. Today, Christina fulfills her desire to travel throughout the world. She believes traveling has impacted her identity and view of the world. By leaving her routine and day-to-day life, she developed her identity.

Christina's key learning is everyone has the privilege of their own opinion. It is our obligation to recognize the gift in diversity of thought. The roots we leave when we travel are the same roots that call us back home at the end of our journey.

After her American experience, Christina attended college in Luzern, Switzerland. After getting her undergraduate degree, she earned a master of law degree. Christina has chosen to be a prosecutor. When asked how she decided her specialty area, she said, "I believe behind every criminal's life is a human being. We are all human, and we all make mistakes."

Christina listens intently to what played into her client's life prior to their arrest. She shared she has learned to listen with an open mind. She says, "It's not easy, and that is a good thing. Challenges are important in life."

I have learned to listen to my heart.
It is difficult to know who is speaking.
Is it my heart or my ego?
I am learning to distinguish
Between
These Two Voices.
—Christina Arnold

Meeting My Bullies Head-On

Dr. Kenneth Libre loves the mountain life, deep-powder skiing, snow safety, and the ski-patrol community. He is the founder of the Alta Medical Clinic, overseeing the needs of visiting tourists, mountain medical emergencies, and his community. Every day, Dr. Libre commutes to work on cross-country skis. He graduated from Geisl School of Medicine, Dartmouth, New Hampshire. He specializes in family medicine. He speaks Spanish and Swedish fluently. His favorite place is to be on the mountain. Dr. Libre lives at Alta, Utah.

Dr. Libre was bullied and teased for his way of speaking and stuttering challenge. He said he is misunderstood by people who talk over him, interrupt him when he is speaking, and treat him poorly. Dr. Libre endeavored to eradicate his stuttering challenge prior to finishing college. He attended several months of speech-therapy camps for two consecutive summers. He came to understand that stuttering was in his DNA. It was neither good nor bad. It was his distinct communication style.

A dean at Dr. Libre's medical school saw beyond the surface of his stuttering speech pattern. She recognized his brilliance and aptitude. She intervened on his behalf when he was discriminated against in the academic arena.

Know when you work hard, you will arrive at your destination. Life is the art of the possible.
—Dr. Kenneth Libre

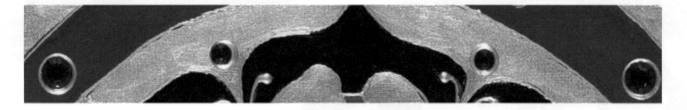

Talking Back to My Inner Critic

Peggy Foster recently gave notice at the Federal Reserve Bank. She was a senior organizational development consultant for the Reserve banking system. She set aside a year to create her dreams in a new home. Motherhood is her greatest and most satisfying job. Now, she was about to move from the history of the home she built with her daughters to a new beginning. The right house eventually found her. She is in the process of redesigning her home for women's retreats focused on well-being integrating yoga and art. Peggy lives in Columbia Heights, Minnesota.

We associate bullies with external negativity from others. It is distinctly possible to be your own bully. In fact, negative self-talk, tearing yourself down, and telling yourself you can't do this or that play into a negative worldview that infects your soul and negatively influences people you come in contact with. Peggy discovered this the hard way. Here is her story, in her own words.

I became my own worst inner critic when I tried out for the Sassy Lassie to be a game show trivia host. For a very long time, the idea had been on my bucket list. Initially when I saw the ad, I realized the auditions had already taken place. I read the bios and saw the pictures of the other hostesses. From the pictures, they looked ten to fifteen years younger than me. My inner critic kicked in. *What are you doing? You are way too old. Plus, it is past the application deadline.*

"Never mind. I am doing it anyway," I shushed my inner critic.

I created an online resume and sent it. To my surprise, the president of the company called and said she would like me to try out. My inner critic was loud and clear. *Just forget it! You can't do this. You will look like a fool!*

I stood ground and said out loud to my inner critic and myself, "It never hurts to try!"

She went to the interview, showed up as herself, and the rest is history! She landed the job as the game show host for a company that puts on trivia parties for large corporations.

Peggy had a big dream to buy a duplex. She divorced and sold the house where her family had been raised. She wanted a different type of house, one that reflected her new start. Her idea was that if she bought a duplex, one side would be her living quarters and the other side would be a retreat center. It would serve as a yoga, art, and coaching center. She searched, but nothing seemed right. She stood in the center of a duplex and could feel an energetic connection.

She put a cash offer on the table and waited. An investor raised the price with his bid. She was disappointed and felt helpless. She said a prayer to God. She believed He did not answer her prayer and was mad at Him for not answering.

Later, she discovered the house had a cracked foundation. To bring the house up to code would have cost an additional $50,000. She stopped being mad at God and was very grateful.

She kept telling herself, "What if my soul wants to be at home wherever I am?" Peggy realized she was looking for a home, not a house.

My biggest achievement in life is joining the Sisterhood of Motherhood.
—Peggy Foster

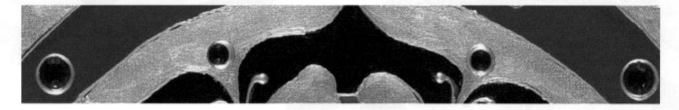

I Faced Mount Everest

Caroline Gleich is the first woman to ski all ninety lines in the Chuting Gallery, a steep skiing guidebook to the Wasatch Range near Salt Lake City, Utah. She has climbed and skied mountain ranges worldwide, including the Alps, the Canadian Rockies, and the Cordillera Blanca. In April 2019, Caroline summited Mount Everest.

Caroline's mission is to inspire people to get outside, live an active lifestyle, and protect the places they love to live and play in. She is a Blue Climate and Oceans Project Ambassador. Caroline graduated Magna Cum Laude, from the University of Utah, with a bachelor of science degree in anthropology.

As a female adventurer in what is still a man's world in the world of mountaineering, Caroline has been challenged with bullying from men who think she doesn't belong on a summit. While critics bother her, she doesn't allow them to dissuade her from undertaking her next adventure.

Caroline's accomplishments have been particularly unusual in the old-guard misogyny and sexist outdoor sporting arena. She speaks and moves with vision and passion. She picks a path and maps out all possibilities to reach her destination. She did this in college, maintaining dean's list status for four years. Caroline's vision and dream have been to become an anthropologist. Her friendly no-nonsense demeanor has supported her quest with great success. Great love with a life partner and having a family are her most personal and highest goals for the future.

Caroline keeps her focus clear and steady with the dreams she has chosen to embrace. Soaring high from a literal perspective is what she does every time she approaches a new climb and skiing descent. Caroline's expertise and courage are evident in the vast array of photoshoots, video parts, and movies she appears in. Caroline demonstrates her strength and recompense to fulfill her dream regardless of the lowly efforts of bullies. This has placed her in a position to be a mentor, leader, and pioneer for women. This has placed her in a unique corporate environment addressing risk management from a perspective of recognizing fear as a central part of processing options to create results.

When frozen with fear, I connect to my meditative state. I listen to my body. I confront my fear.
—Caroline Gleich

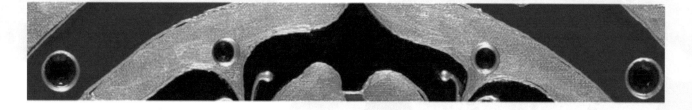

Great Questions to Ask

- Who are the bullies blocking your flight?
- How do you feel when they show up?
- How do you respond?

_____

_____

_____

_____

_____

_____

_____

_____

_____

_____

_____

_____

_____

_____

_____

_____

Themes, Core Concepts, and Lessons Learned

- Bullies block your path to protect their insecurity.
- Surround yourself with a community of people who champion you.
- Be your own advocate.

Chapter Notes and Resources

Five common tactics bullies use to extort undue influence and power are:

1. Physical bullying
2. Tangible/material bullying
3. Verbal bullying
4. Passive aggressive or covert bullying
5. Cyber bullying

There are four actions people can draw on to protect themselves: stand tall, ask others to witness, create a paper trail, and seek professional advice.

Ni, Preston. "Five Ways That Adult Bully Each Other." *Psychology Today*, January 22, 2017.

CHAPTER 8

What If Your Landing Is Not on Your Radar?

The dreams we think we want show up much different from what we imagined. In that moment we are surprised It is exactly what we desired.
—Ruth M. Godfrey

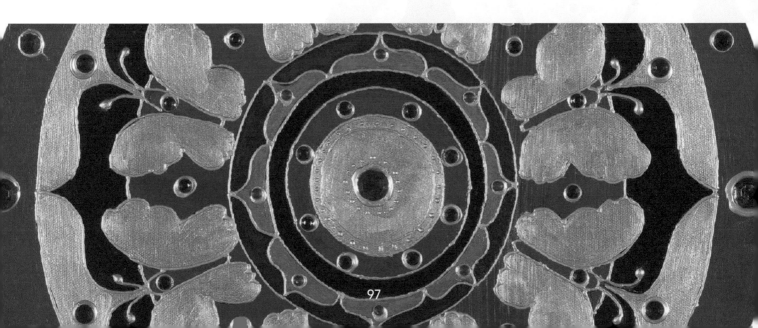

97

Mandala and The Butterfly

Experiencing a mandala is like having to file a flight plan more than once. The purpose of the experience is to notice the space in between. The process allows for change, unexpected outcomes, and new perspectives.

This is significant as you recognize your dreams. The horizon is in the distance; sometimes you may find yourself off your radar. Look to the butterfly's symbolism to gather strength in the unknown. Trust your path is clear, holding one destination with many routes to choose from.

When you are not attached to the outcome, the results will surprise you. The path of your dream flights are limited by expectations. The outcome is unknown, requiring trust. It moves you to recognize the important parts of your life. It gives you time to reflect on the details of your life. How can you celebrate your landing? The following stories can answer the question. The first story is from Ginnymarie.

I Lost My Friend

He had the deepest brown-black hair, thick and wavy, eyelashes flapping like butterfly wings. His dark brown eyes smiled. I met him through a friend snowboarding at Snowbird Ski and Summer Resort.

The following summer, I traveled to Santiago, Chile, with a group of friends on a ski adventure. We stayed in the first lodge built in La Parva, Chile. Its heat source was the original stone fireplace. The managers in the lodge spoke German and Spanish. Communication was difficult. My Spanish was limited. My three years of German classes several decades ago did not serve me well.

It was early morning. We sat eating our Euro-style breakfast when the lodge manager came looking for me. There was a phone call. On the other end of the line was my Chilean friend. He offered to bring me to his resort for the day, ride the mountain, and meet his fiancée. I spent a week backcountry skiing and mountaineering with my Chilean friends. I said if he could get back to the States by winter, he could join our team at my Snowbird Ski and Summer Resort jewelry store, Canyon Designs Jewelry and Objets d'Art.

December rolled in. I opened the door one morning, there in the entryway stood my friend. True to my word, I now had a Chilean friend working in my store. He learned to do and be the best sales associate.

Our winter was extraordinary. Snow levels were high, making backcountry riding dangerous. The avalanche forecasters warned people to stay out of the backcountry. My friend disregarded the warnings. He went to the backcountry to ride the new powder. Each time, I asked, "Do you have your avalanche transponders, and are the batteries fresh? Have you taken the recommended avalanche training courses?"

My Chilean friend would smile and say, "Yes, of course."

Spring came and with it corn conditions. Corn snow is soft and forgiving. It is not too wet or slushy. It is called the "Goldilocks of snow"—not too hard, not too soft, just right. Corn conditions beckon people to travel into the backcountry without proper knowledge and equipment.

It was a chaotic morning at the store. Afternoon came, with more warnings from the Utah Avalanche Center alerting people to extreme conditions. My phone rang. It was the county sheriff's department. They asked if I was Ginnymarie Leines.

"Yes?" I said.

The sheriff told me my friend had died in an avalanche the previous hour. He requested that I identify his body. Later, I was asked to provide my friends dress clothes for the mortuary. I was in a state of shock. I gathered Atillo's black dress shirt, trousers, and tie. My friend was laid out on a gurney with a sheet covering him. The mortician lifted the sheet so I could see his face. There he was, at peace, smiling with his thick, long, curly eyelashes. He was gone. Nothing we could do would bring him back.

I stood paralyzed. My spirit felt broken for his fiancée, his family, and his twin brother. We held a memorial service at the resort near the site of the avalanche. His friends spoke of his great love for adventure, his kindness, and his generosity.

Several months later, working at my shop, I was alone. I needed and wanted to be comforted by my family.

I could not reach out and tell them my need. I felt compelled to be a strong mother. My three sons were involved in big mountain adventures with avalanche danger and changing snow conditions daily.

I wish I could return to that moment in time without losing my friend.

—Ginnymarie

My Bipolar Bear

Dave Richards rises long before the sun. In the winter, he wakes at 3:15 a.m. to begin his day. He strategizes and plans for the safety of the people who come to ski at the Alta Ski Area. Dave carries the responsibility of mitigating avalanche danger with his Ski Patrol Crew using artillery, hand charges, and Gas-X technology. Dave is a caring friend who listens and shares questions about life's deeper mysteries. Dave enjoys river kayaking and camping in the summer. He is the director of snow safety, avalanche forecasting, a snow science expert, a ski patroller, and an educational and inspirational speaker. Dave lives at Alta, Utah.

As a child growing up with freedom to explore the mountain wilderness; Dave developed mountaineering skills that would plant him in a place of great leadership and responsibility. What followed him as a child was something he called "the bear." It was a predatory animal creating havoc with his brain chemistry, later diagnosed as bipolar disorder.

Dave's landing was on his radar. "The Bear" was not. As a sought-after avalanche forecaster, snow safety director, and director of ski patrol, Dave has managed to live his dream while contending with a lifelong challenge.

Dave has created a format to integrate his professional life with his private challenge, living with a bipolar brain. Dave has inspired new paradigms of evaluations, interaction, and balance within medical, educational, and community services. He has suffered. He has cried out in strangulating distress. He has fought the battle. He has learned how to live with the known and unknown as the Bear walks alongside him. Dave lives his dream every day.

I Have Learned That
What I Do
is Not Who I am.
Nothing is Worth Doing
to the Point Of,
Losing the One I Love.
"Now I AM ALONE"
—Dave Richards

I Healed Within

Kristin Burich is an energy healer. She is a National Board certified colonic hydrotherapist and holds an endermologie certification. Kristin is a computer programmer. Her bachelor of science degree is from the University of Minnesota, in computer science, with minors in chemistry, biology, and math. Kristin lives in Woodbury, Minnesota.

At the age of four, Kristin experienced humiliation and demeaning treatment. From that time on, she felt she needed to prove to the world how smart she is. Kristin made a vow to herself. For the next forty-plus years, she focused on scientific academics. Kristin has a sense of calm that supersedes every form of chaos. Her quiet, joyful energy reflects humility with a deep fountain of sage wisdom and resourcefulness. She walked away from a career of academic validation to a dream that brought her into an unexpected landing zone.

Kristen opened Healing Within Wellness Center in 2002. Her mission focuses on providing a platform to gain balance and harmony of the body-soul connection for her clients. Kristin's passion and joy comes from working with people on their healing path. She draws on energy work, colonic hydrotherapy, and sound therapy modalities for her clients.

Shifting into the healing energy field has illuminated itself to be very similar to the understanding of computers for her. This parallel has served Kristin, and her dream became vividly clear when she chose to accept her new landing zone. The courage to step out of her academic paradigm into a completely new and different field brought her where she is today. Kristin reminded us it is important to ask yourself, *What is in my highest good?* The human tendency is similar to our disliking change, but it involves more a commitment to take action than trying to avoid change.

The best thing you can give to the world is joy.
—Kristin Burich

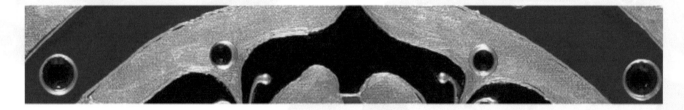

Great Questions to Ask

- What if your landing is not on your radar?
- What will you do if your radar system fails?
- How will this new landing impact your dreams?

_____

_____

_____

_____

_____

_____

_____

_____

_____

_____

_____

_____

_____

_____

_____

_____

_____

Themes, Core Concepts, and Lessons Learned

- Trust your landing is exactly where you're supposed to be.
- Provide an important pause to reassess.
- Find meaning and purpose in your dreams.

Chapter Notes and Resources

The privilege of a lifetime is being who you are. Expectation creates disappointment. When our landing is not where our radar directs us, we often feel lost. In these cases, we can choose to observe this is the life that has found us. We must be willing to get rid of the life we've planned so as to accept the life that is waiting for us.

Campbell, Joseph. Campbell Companion: *Reflections on the Art of Living*. New York: Harper Perennial Publishers, 1991.

CHAPTER 9

What If Becoming Is the Soul of Your Journey?

When Dawn has Me Ready Triggered
to Launch
my Fevered Dream.
I Call This
The Dream, Dreaming Me."
—Tim Boyle

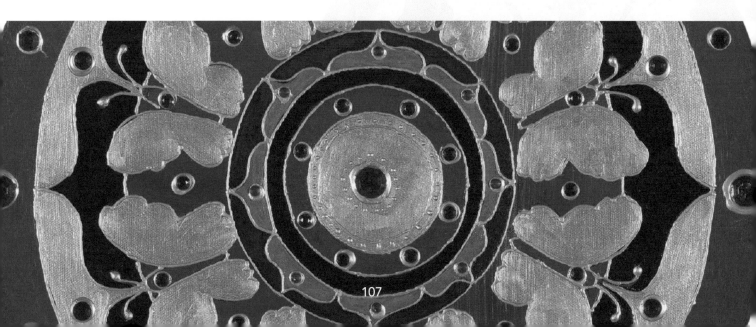

Mandala and The Butterfly

The fascinating mystery of the mandala is the soulful journey it offers you. The essence of the mandala's encounter is parallel to your dream journey. The reality is the world is in constant motion, change, and renewal. When you choose to dance in the moment, just as the chrysalis moves toward transformation, you will be filled with hope and knowing. The butterfly is filled with trust during the chrysalis stage. It will be transformed into a butterfly. The mandala and butterfly carry messages deep within themselves. The mandala has a unique message for you as you gaze into its mystery. Distraction is not an option for the butterfly, and the mandala invites you to awaken and recognize your message.

You can choose to see, feel, and hear the message. It can be carried and acted upon with hope and courage. It is yours when you recognize and act on your dreams. The butterfly has a message for you to carry as well. It carries a message telling you to take flight with hope and courage.

Dreams Become YOU

Your experiences have the power to call you to your true self. It is a sacred process of becoming when you wake up to your call. It takes you on a heartfelt journey. What journey is calling you at this moment?

The messages you now carry are filled with possibility. They remind you to trust who you are. They provide you with your answers. They are your dreams to act on.

We have discovered persistent nudging signals to take flight. Trusting your inner knowing creates the possibility to enter into your dreams. At this moment, fear often shows up. It can be a powerful force if you allow it to be. Recognize when you are blocked by fear. It gives you time to feel.

Bullies can be the unexpected, playing a significant role in sabotaging your dreams. Be aware of the negative people around you who do not want you to achieve your dreams. They get pleasure seeing you struggle. You may find you need to separate yourself from negative people before you can continue your journey.

In Paulo Coelho's *The Alchemist*, the merchant tells the shepherd boy, "You are forcing me to look at … horizons I have never known."

Your dream journeys can take you into unknown places, bringing you to a new landing. You have become the soul of your journey.

Dreams give you courage to act. They are your hope for your future. As you contemplate your way forward, consider these illustrative stories from people who have made a journey before you. The first story is from Ruthie.

My Conflict with Inner and Outer Beauty

As a young girl, I was confused as to how inner beauty shows up. Clearly, I didn't know. My grandmother and mother had strong opinions about what that meant. I don't think they knew, either.

Their view of beauty began with hair.

My grandmother plopped me down on her kitchen stool. "Sit still," she would say. She tied my hair in rags. Twisting and turning throughout the night, I'd wake up with rags falling out of my hair. There were no curls. My grandmother was not happy.

I wanted my grandmother's approval. I decided to try harder to become beautiful for her.

I didn't have much time to master beauty. My grandmother passed away when I was six years old. The task of beautifying me fell on the shoulders of my mother. Mother's views were like my grandmother's.

"It all begins with your hair," she would say. The rags were tossed out the window. Mother moved onto a sophisticated beauty method—or so she thought. Mother's new doctrine left me at the mercy of permanents. I was her guinea pig before she tried new beauty products on her clientele.

Mother was intent on creating curly hair. My brothers had a unique way of letting me know how much perms stunk up our house. I can see John and Tom pinching their noses with clothespins. They stuck their tongues out at me and covered their ears, teasing me.

My father didn't help. He would ask, "Ruthie, do you know how to use a comb?"

"Why?" I would ask.

His immediate response was, "Well, I was just wondering because one hair seems to be chasing another." He walked away laughing.

At age nine, beauty took on a new meaning for me. It became a color—the color white. My aunts were very excited. They could now buy me a First Communion outfit. I had white shoes, a white dress, a white veil, white socks, and yes, white undies. The nuns told the girls at our school we were to wear white on our First Communion day. It was to be a symbol of our inner beauty and purity. The year was filled with study and preparation for the coming event. The Sacraments were to give me a different view of beauty.

Sister Helen Clair talked about our inner soul. She would say, "Our soul is the only thing that matters. It allows people to see your inner beauty. This is when you will become the girl God has sent you to earth to be."

Sister Helen Clair created a different image of beauty for me. She planted the seeds of who I would become.

I had flunked the path of external beauty—especially if it really did start with hair. The idea of inner beauty was put on the backburner by our school principal, Sister Loretta. I wanted to become a nun. She gently took me by the hand, saying, "Oh, honey, we just aren't ready for you." Until then, I was certain I possessed Sister Helen Claire's inner beauty.

Years later, my mother declared there was new hope for me. She found an advertisement at Dayton's Department Store. Dayton's was offering an eight-week class for teens on the proper way to become a young lady.

My mother was elated. I thought it was the dumbest idea. It wasn't long after her idea came to fruition. I found myself sitting at Dayton's Charm School. My friend Marie took the class with me. She was thrilled with the whole idea. I never was sure why.

The instructors took their roles seriously. We had a homework assignment each week. I couldn't believe it. We had to practice walking with a book balanced on our head each night. Slouching was unacceptable. We were told this would create attention and make us beautiful. We had to learn how to set a table with fine china, flowers, a tablecloth, and the trimmings. I wondered what it had to do with becoming beautiful. My mom loved the idea that her oldest daughter finally knew how to set the table properly. She enjoyed signing off on my homework.

Each student created a scrapbook of women they thought were beautiful. I wondered what the criteria was.

Graduation would signify we were ready to go out in the world with manners and charm. We prepared for the Dayton's Sky Room Style Show.

The prospects of modeling and wearing two different outfits went to my head. I was going to be a model.

I thought I had mastered the runway protocol. I imagined myself as a famous model. I stood for hours in front of my long mirror in my bedroom, gazing at myself.

The day of the style show, I was nervous, afraid I had forgotten everything I had learned. I walked the runway, tripping over an electrical cord. One thing I did correctly was stand tall. Walking with the book balanced on my head paid off, but eight weeks of intense study did not make me beautiful.

This was not my mother's first attempt to make her daughter beautiful. At my dance recital at age five, she pulled me off the stage, embarrassed, and said, "You have two left feet." This time, I was a teenager. I was way too big to be pulled off the stage. I told my mom not to worry; "I have two sisters you can work on."

It was not until much later in life I revisited the importance of inner beauty. I now realize true beauty reflects our inner soul. I can see this in the way I treat myself. It is reflected in the way I have fallen in love with my life. My inner love is reflected outwardly to share with the world. The mystery that escapes me is, even today, *I wonder if my mother saw this in me?*

The reality is my grandmother and mother were wrong. It was never about hair. Dayton's Sky Room classes were wrong too. It was never about balancing books on my head, walking the runway or setting a perfect table. It was about reflecting the inner beauty of my soul shared with the world around me.

—Ruthie

What the Caterpillar Calls
The End,
The rest of the World
Calls a Butterfly.
—Lao Tzu

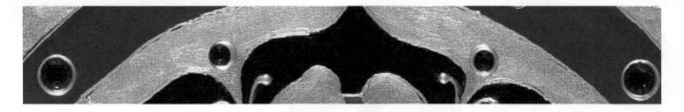

My Soul Is the Mountain

A world-renowned competitive snowboarder, Bjorn Jon Leines has been voted "Top Ten Best Rider of All Time." He has been the most photographed snowboarder on the planet for many years. He is the winner of Rider of the Year, and a top finisher at the US Open and Nationals. He was an Olympic qualifier for the 1998 Winter Games and a US National Team member. He is an X Games medalist. Bjorn has been a X Games commentator. He is an entrepreneur, cofounder of CELTEK, and founder and owner of OVAN Eyewear. He is vice president and an owner of Cardiff Snowcraft. Bjorn is married to Kristin. They have two sons, Bearakhan and Micaiah Ryder. They live in Salt Lake City, Utah.

Self-awareness has shaped Bjorn's life. His dreams burned brightly at a young age. He folded towels and matched socks for a year to save up for his first snowboard. Bjorn's vivid imagination and visualization of his dreams have brought him to where he is today. Here is his story.

The DHC-2 Beaver Bush Plane circled, then circled deeper into the Canadian interior's wilderness before the weather closed in. The Forum team riders arrived at the abandoned mining camp in the Yukon wilderness.

Daylight appeared as the storm moved in, erasing visibility. The pilot, videographer, photographer, and riders grabbed their backpacks and made their way from the chopper to a cabin.

The movie *Video Gangs* would become the result of their arduous ten days of heavy snow, extreme avalanche danger, and an emaciated pack of howling gray wolves. They paced back and forth outside their cabin. The cabin became a refuge and a lockdown. The weather settled in. Day after day, they checked satellite weather forecasts. There was no end to the snowfall and high wind warnings.

Day ten—the last day of their trip and the day to fly out—rose with a blue sky and nine feet of light, fluffy, and dangerous snow. Saving time and getting footage in the can created a momentum of pressure to get the shot on the first flyover.

Knowing snow conditions would continue to shift and calve into avalanches, they chose a safe zone to get their footage. Riding on the ski basket strapped into his snowboard, bracing against the fuselage and gripping the basket grate was Bjorn's helicopter lift up the mountain. Hovering over the peak, positioned for a launch, Bjorn jumped away from the basket, landing thirty feet below, making a controlled carve to bullet himself toward the ninety-foot feature they had chosen earlier in the morning.

Each time he rode toward the helicopter, he ducked his head with blades whirling sandblasting now crystalizing on his goggles. He hung on tight, and the ground dropped off under him. He thought about his next leap from the basket to charge down to the jump with speed and control. Plan A was to do big mountain riding. They were fully immersed in plan B, with Mother Nature entirely in charge.

Their human ingenuity and the "oh, sh—t" factor pushed them forward. Several lifts later, they had the footage in the can, and they played one last game of rock, paper, scissors to see who got the last drop before they would be ferried back to the airfield, homeward bound. Bjorn was awarded Best Rider of the Year by his peers, Best Video Part of the Year by *Transworld* magazine, and Top Best Rider of All Time by his peers. The Volcom movie *Escramble* points to his environmental awareness.

Bjorn is a reflective visionary who has chosen his life path in his early teen years. He has learned to listen to his heart and intuition before making decisions. As a young boy, he dreamed of becoming a professional snowboarder. His dreams have become his reality. They have determined his place within the global community. His dream has created circles of communities that span cultures, friendships, business, and industries. Bjorn believed his dream was possible, and it proved to be true. His dreams became much bigger than he imagined, creating a complete sense of belonging in the world.

It happened because I believed it could happen.
—Bjorn Jon Leines

How My Life Is a Miracle

Dave Powers writes an unofficial snow report each day for all people interested in Snowbird Ski and Summer Resort's mountain conditions. His writing is entertaining and eccentric, embellished with terms that he coins. He calls his women friends at the resort "Shredtastic Ladies of Power" and encourages them to speed safely. Dave can be followed at gurudavepowers.com. Dave's planetary office is at the Forklift Restaurant on the Plaza at Snowbird. He can be contacted there daily between 10:30 and 11:30 a.m. Skiers and snowboarders come in to consult about the best powder stashes and runs on the mountain. Dave has been on his mission for forty years. He skis six days a week, from the first day the resort is open to the very last day of the season. He often posts pictures of interesting and unique people who seek him out, sharing their stories. He is coauthor of *Snowbird Secrets: A Guide to Big Mountain Skiing*. Dave lives in Salt Lake City, Utah.

For Dave, skiing is his passion, and he has spent much of his life involved in the sport. That didn't happen by accident. He actively pursued his desire to ski to his heart's content. He let go of his fears and anxieties. Instead, he let magic and wonder take control, and his dreams became a reality. Here is his story.

Making turn after turn, 1,500 feet of vertical fell away, as did the snow, forming an undulating pattern from his descent behind him. It was another gift of the snow Mother Nature, creating a 24-inch bank of 6 percent water flakes, calling out to come and ravish its majesty. This is a moment in time Dave shares as he approaches Snowbird Ski Resorts Hidden Peak more than one hundred days a season. He offers his mountain conquests, observations, and glee on his blog, *Guru Dave's Snow Report*. Thousands of followers read his snow report every day.

If he is not to be found on the mountain, he can be found in the hearts and minds of Snowbird locals and international aficionados. Written daily, it promises a menagerie of ethereal and esoteric experiences quantifying the magic of riding the mountain in awe and wonder of its command. Dave's sense of his planetary purpose and quiet joy is strong. His willingness to seek knowledge and understanding at a deep spiritual and metaphysical level is evident in his mountain experience. He has a ritual of skiing, observing, feeling, and celebrating the mystery as he skis turn after turn.

Conversing with Dave is like going on a magical mystery tour of possibility based in the moment. Dave stands strong in his belief system and study, illuminating the Course in Miracles and the Course in Love.

He has been studying these courses for forty years. His big-picture vision is for peace on earth. He shared when we create issues that are not of our concern, we bring negativity into our lives. This is a profound reminder of how we affect the journeys of our souls.

When I work from the heart, the good, the exact perfect place calls me to walk the path, allowing source to manifest my life instead of me.
—Dave Powers

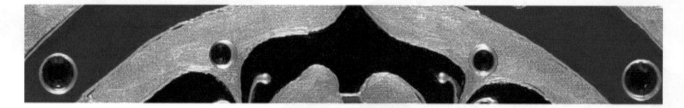

Be still.
Be discerning.
Be trusting.
Become your dreams.

The number nine is all about the discovery and fulfillment of your life dreams. It is a magical number, and the nine chapters of *Mandala and the Butterfly* symbolize completion and fulfillment to experience your dreams. You possess the courage to move forward on your journey of self-discovery. Now you have the power to take action. Once you do, everything will fall into place. You'll find an enhanced connection to yourself and the universe and the happiness that comes with it. You can affect change in your life. You are on your way to doing just that! Congratulations!

Life is not measured by the number of breaths you take but by the moments that take your breath away.

—Author unknown, disputed sources

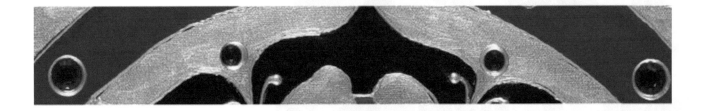

Great Questions to Ask

- Who are you becoming?
- How are your experiences creating your soulful journey?
- What moments give your dreams flight?

_____

_____

_____

_____

_____

_____

_____

_____

_____

_____

_____

_____

_____

_____

_____

Themes, Core Concepts, and Lessons Learned

- Becoming is a sacred journey.
- We wake up when we respond to our dreams.
- Name your dreams, claim them, own them, express them.

Chapter Notes and Resources

Dr. Brené Brown discovered in her extensive Delte here are four powerful elements of true belonging, which are highlighted below. We included them for you as these practices provide the ability to *become*.

1. People are hard to hate close up. Move in.
2. Speak truth to bullshit. Be civil.
3. Hold hands with strangers.
4. Soft front, strong back, wild heart.

Brown, Brené. *Braving the Wilderness*. New York: Random House Publishing, 2017.

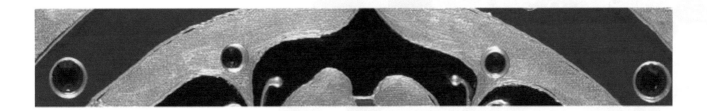

I Have Become My Dreams

I am the new world,
Gazing into your eyes,
I have become still.
I have become discerning.
I have become trusting.
I have become my dreams.
This is my power.

I see the setting sun,
The rising moon,
The night sky,
The first whispers of dawn.
It is the same majesty
To behold,
Yesterday, today, tomorrow.
I have found the majesty in
My new world.
It is quiet.

I am love.
I am possibility.
I have become my dreams.

—Ginnymarie M. Leines

ACKNOWLEDGMENTS

Writing and publishing this book unfolded over the course of four years. The process wove a tapestry of stories shared from the heart. With gratitude, we feel blessed each contributor gave their time to us. Their unique stories bring light to the challenges and victories of listening to and following our awakening dreams with hope and courage.

Thank you to our early readers for their insights and thoughts as follows:

Dr. Alice Woog, Jennie Antolak, Mitzi Dunford, Barbie Ingram, Caren Nemec, Doug Blake, Darci Watson, Tracy Off, Paul Heussenstamm, my soulmate husband Gregory, and the students and graduates of The International School of Coaching, Learning Journeys. We extend an extraordinary thank-you to our families and friends who listened and encouraged us on our journey.

ABOUT THE AUTHORS

Ruth Godfrey is the founder of the International Center of Coaching, Learning Journeys, which she co-owns with her daughter, Jennie Antolak. Exploring the ideas of <u>Mandala and The Butterfly</u> has been a creative structural placeholder for her. The writing experience continually reminded her of the importance of breathing life into dreams. She lives in Woodbury, Minnesota. She has three adult children and five precocious grandchildren. Her wish for all readers is to become the soul of their journeys, allowing their dreams to take flight. The following are some of her professional credentials: Master of Science, Adult and Occupational Education, Kansas State University, Bachelor of Science, Recreational Leadership, University of Minnesota, master certified coach, designated by the International Coach Federation; certified narrative coach practitioner. She is the co-author of *Delicious Conversations and Coach on the Run 10: A Way of Being.*

www.learningjourneys.net

Curious, inquisitive, and a seeker of the mysteries and adventures of life, Ginnymarie M. Leines is a master certified coach and narrative coach practitioner from the International Center of Coaching, Learning Journeys. She loves people, listening to their stories, and delighting in their vision and possibility. A businesswoman, entrepreneur, international manufacturer, designer, artist, and educator; she is the mother of three sons and three daughters (in-law), grandmother to eight grandchildren, and lover of Gregory her soulmate, partner, and husband of fifty years. She lives at Alta, Utah. The following are some of her professional credentials: Bachelor of Science, Language Arts, English, Secondary Education, Journalism, and Communciation, Hamline University, St. Paul, Minnesota. University of Minnesota, Leadership Training Certification, Seven Habits of Highly Effective People, Shirlaws Business Coach.

www.ginnymarieleines.com

Printed in the United States
by Baker & Taylor Publisher Services